Evangelism
in a
Changing America

Evangelism
in a
Changing America

By Jesse M. Bader

The Bethany Press

St. Louis, Mo.

269
B14e

35962
Feb. '58

Copyright 1957

by

The Bethany Press

Library of Congress Catalog Card Number 57-8364

Printed in the United States of America

DEDICATED

TO THE

DEPARTMENT OF EVANGELISM

OF THE

NATIONAL COUNCIL OF THE CHURCHES OF CHRIST
IN THE UNITED STATES OF AMERICA

This book had its beginning in a meeting of the Committee on Evangelism of the Home and State Missions Planning Council of Disciples of Christ while Thomas W. Toler, St. Joseph, Missouri, was chairman. The Committee long felt that a book on evangelism by an authority, as Dr. Bader has become, would be welcome in many places. He was most cooperative in preparing this tremendous labor of love and this book carries the wholehearted endorsement of every member of this committee.

G. GERALD SIAS, Enid, Oklahoma, chairman
DAVID S. MCNELLY, Indianapolis, Indiana, secretary

James L. Ballinger, Indianapolis, Indiana
John Chenault, Frankfort, Kentucky
Ira Crewdson, Little Rock, Arkansas
Chester Crow, Fort Worth, Texas
John W. Frye, Indianapolis, Indiana
Newell M. Hall, Vincennes, Indiana
J. R. Johnson, Shawnee, Oklahoma
Mrs. Chloe Kelly, Cleveland, Ohio
Dan C. Kenner, Little Rock, Arkansas
Ephraim D. Lowe, Indianapolis, Indiana
William H. McKinney, Indianapolis, Indiana
Charles W. Ross, Macon, Georgia
Frank C. Rustemeyer, Memphis, Tennessee
William Martin Smith, Indianapolis, Indiana
Vernon Stout, Pittsfield, Illinois
Thomas Underwood, Prairie Village, Kansas
R. W. Wallace, Indianapolis, Indiana

PREFACE

After twelve years as the Secretary of Evangelism for the United Christian Missionary Society of Disciples of Christ and twenty years as the Executive Secretary of Evangelism for the former Federal Council of Churches and three years as the Executive Director of Evangelism for the National Council of Churches, I have finally found time to write a book. After thirty-five years in this full-time work in evangelism, I present with considerable humility a book on the work to which I have given some of the most fruitful years of my life.

No writer can possibly exhaust the theme of evangelism in one book. Many important matters must be left out and many phases of this, the greatest work in the world, must be omitted. However, I have tried to present and discuss what seem to be the basic essentials in evangelism with reference to motive, method, and message.

The book has been written for interdenominational use. I hope all members of all communions may find some suggestions and inspiration in the book. Also, I have had pastors, laymen, and laywomen in mind, as the book has been prepared. The author expresses the hope that the book may be of value to students and faculties in Bible colleges and seminaries. Also, the book has been written specifically for America and with the American scene in mind.

I am indebted to many persons for help in writing this book. Many friends have made valuable suggestions with reference to the scope, content, and use of the book. If the book helps pastors, the laity, and youth in our American churches in this primary work for Christ and the church—which is evangelism—I shall be greatly pleased.

Jesse M. Bader

CONTENTS

INTRODUCTION

When the tides turned against evangelism in the "roaring 20's," Jesse M. Bader was just beginning a life dedicated to the promulgation of the Great Commission of Christ. In 1920 he became the first full-time Secretary of Evangelism for Disciples of Christ. When other church leaders were turning away from the word "evangelism," Jesse M. Bader was seeking to discover new meaning and purpose in this word, as well as new methods by which to evangelize. He has been one of the leaders instrumental in bringing about a complete cycle of events, and has literally turned the tide from antievangelism to a spirit most favorable today for evangelism.

In 1932 Dr. Bader succeeded the late Dr. Charles L. Goodell as Secretary of Evangelism of the Federal Council of the Churches of Christ in America and was executive director of the Joint Department of Evangelism within the organization of the National Council of the Churches of Christ in America until his retirement in 1954. At the time of retirement he had given thirty-four years to the actual administrative work of planning and promoting the work of evangelism in America.

Most men who retire write a book of memories. Jesse M. Bader has written a book of "marching orders." Many men write books; but no man has ever more completely lived the book he has written than Jesse M. Bader in his *Evangelism in a Changing America.*

9

He has outthought, outworked and outloved his contemporaries, to turn the tide of religion in America toward a great revival. His passion for evangelism, his zeal for ecumenicity, his compassion for the misguided, and his love on behalf of the unlovely, as well as his concern for the unconcerned, has excelled in every circle on the American church scene. Dr. Bader has moved across America and many kindred nations in the last quarter of a century, breathing the evangelistic spirit of life into the church, making bold the Great Commission of Jesus Christ. Few men in this century have done as much to proclaim salvation and establish the convert.

The Committee on Evangelism of the Home and State Missions Planning Council of the Disciples of Christ have urged Dr. Bader to write this book, because we felt no living man among us in Christendom has done so much to lead so many to effective evangelism. This book is a witness to a bold fact of Dr. Bader's life, i.e., when he moved into a community, men of all faiths moved closer together, and through his leadership, churches of all shades of Christian belief were brought to realize that the task they all had in common was to proclaim the Great Commission of our Christ. Through evangelism, Jesse M. Bader created a united witness in many a community where all other religious appeals had failed.

A quarter of a century ago men were critical of his methods and techniques in evangelism—today many patterns of evangelism used by the American church were pioneered, perfected, and promoted first by Dr. Bader. He has stood with the stalwarts and has done as much as any living man to establish a climate for evangelism in America today.

Through his book he lives and breathes, speaks and bears witness to the power of the Great Commission and thus proclaims the challenge of the unfinished task of our Lord, Jesus Christ—"Go into all the world."

This is not a book by a man whose work is done, but a book with the freshness of a man who has just begun. He writes as he speaks and lives—*Evangelism in a Changing America.*

> DAVID S. MCNELLY, *Associate Secretary and Director of Evangelism, The Department of Church Development and Evangelism, The United Christian Missionary Society, Disciples of Christ, Indianapolis, Indiana*

CHAPTER 1

COMPULSIONS TO EVANGELIZE

Evangelism is not the only business of the church but it is the church's first business and what Jesus Christ made primary his church dare not make secondary. Evangelism is not an elective. It is a divine imperative. The church must evangelize or perish. There is no alternative. To evangelize is the greatest work in the world. What spring is to the earth; what sunshine is to flowers; what a physician is to the sick; what a boat is to a drowning man, true evangelism is to a lost soul and a sinful world.

This word "evangelism" is one of the most significant words in the vocabulary of the church. It is a dynamic word, filled with heartthrobs, drumbeats, and trumpet sounds. Up to the present time, no one has been able to find a significant substitute for it. It is highly probable that no substitute will ever be found to supplant this word, which means so much to Christians all over the world.

However, there are some here and there within the church today who are allergic to the word. It is my observation that their numbers are growing fewer and fewer. One reason why some shun the use of the word is because the business of evangelism is so exacting and demanding upon a Christian. Also, because the real meaning and purpose is sometimes misunderstood. In the minds of some, evangelism and revivalism have been made synonymous. A revival meeting is only one method of evangelism and not evangelism itself. There is a vast difference between real New Testament evangelism and the many methods used to carry it on.

What is evangelism? It is impossible to find a definition that adequately expresses its real and comprehensive meaning. It has been attempted often and perhaps it is a good thing for each generation of Christians to attempt its own definition as to the meaning of this word. To me the best and most comprehensive definition is the one that was formulated by the representatives of thirty Protestant communions at the time of the Columbus, Ohio, meeting of the Executive Committee of the Federal Council of Churches in 1946. After much prayer and considerable discussion, the Department of Evangelism of the Council recommended this definition which was unanimously adopted. It reads, Evangelism is "The presentation of the Good News of God in Jesus Christ, so that men are brought, through the power of the Holy Spirit, to put their trust in God; accept Jesus Christ as their Savior from the guilt and power of sin; follow and serve Him as their Lord in the fellowship of the Church and in the vocations of the common life." Up to now, no individual, congregation, or communion has come forward with a suggested revision of this Columbus definition or has recommended a substitute for it. This definition is worth memorizing. It could well become the basis for a sermon or a lecture on evangelism.

This word "evangelism" contains another word. It is the word "evangel," which means *good news* or *momentous tidings.* We call it the *gospel.* The Greek word for gospel is *euangelion,* which is the root of the word "evangelism." This evangel we preach and teach is as fresh as the break of day and as old as the continuity of daybreak through the ages. Like its author Jesus Christ, it is the same yesterday, today, and forever. It grows not yellow with age. Time does not abate its power nor dim its glory. The Apostle Paul, the intrepid evangelist of the New Testament, said of this evangel, "I am not ashamed of the gospel: it is the power of God for salvation to everyone who has faith, to the Jew first and also to the Greek." (Romans 1:16.)

The evangel is the "good news" about God's nature, purpose, power, and love. Since God is not to be classified with any other reality, the gospel of and about him is unique. The whole Christian movement rests upon this eternal evangel, which is from God and not from men. Much of the loss of power to evangelize on the part of Christians and churches today is due to the loss of this conception of the uniqueness of the evangel, which is related to the nature, purpose, and power of the one true living God for persons and for mankind everywhere. There can be no evangelism without the everlasting evangel of God as revealed in Jesus Christ.

There is a compulsion about evangelism. There is a force in it that drives and compels Christians to engage in this sublime task. There is a restlessness in this word. It pushes the followers of Christ out into the white harvest fields of the world "to make disciples." Evangelism in the heart of Paul made of him a tireless winner of souls, who said, "I have become all things to all men, that I might by all means save some." (1 Corinthians 9:22.) In the heart of John Wesley it caused him to give himself unreservedly for the salvation of England. In the life of John Knox it led him to exclaim, "Give me Scotland or I die." Dwight L. Moody experienced the compulsion of evangelism in his own life, so much so that it urged him on and on to the last ounce of his strength. These and many others through the centuries have been kept at the work of evangelism in season and out of season, because of their desire to make Christ known, loved, and obeyed.

In many churches today there is a tragic lack of concern for the winning of others to Christ. The sense of urgency is gone. A local congregation is always in danger of becoming a chubby, clubby, complacent collection of nice folks—a sort of closed shop for the edification of the saints. Because of a lack of concern and sense of urgency to be found in a number of churches, there are few if any in their respective communities who are brought into the membership of the church. The best methods, the finest machinery, and the latest literature are all impotent unless there is a burning desire and a great passion to win others to Christ and the church. Our Lord said of himself, "The Son of man came to seek and to save the lost." (Luke 19:10.) He never allowed himself to forget why he came, for he was always seeking and he was always saving. Those who would be his disciples must share his concern and passion for the lost.

Evangelism when taken seriously disturbs complacent Christians and motivates comfortable churches into action. These compulsions come upon each Christian and every church from two directions—from without, like the force of water that falls upon a millwheel, and from within, like the power generated from an electric motor.

The Compulsions from Without

These compulsions from without come upon Christians and churches in three ways. They come silently, yet insistently and forcefully, when once the passion for winning souls burns upon the altar of the heart.

The Command of Christ—Among the last words of Christ to his disciples while he was on earth were these, "Go therefore and make disciples of all nations, baptizing them in the name of the Father and of the Son and of the Holy Spirit." (Matthew 28:19.) This word from him who said, "All authority in heaven and on earth has been given to me" (Matthew 28:18), is not a suggestion. It is an imperative. It is a command from the King of kings and the Lord of lords. The last words of our loved ones are usually cherished most and remembered longest. If, perchance, they have left any requests, we are only too glad to comply with them and carry them out if at all possible. These words of the Great Commission are among Christ's last words. Surely Christians in any generation cannot forget them or slight them.

The early Christians took this evangelistic imperative seriously. They put everything they had into it—time, possessions, and life itself. They counted not their lives as dear unto themselves. As we read our New Testament, we note that nothing happened easily in the early church. Everything was difficult. Someone has described it this way, "Every footprint in the Book of Acts is stained with blood." Christians, in the first three centuries, multiplied rapidly. Their motto in those early days seemed to be, "We tell it; they believe it; Christ does it." They seemed to say by their lives and their message, "We tell it—that is our business. They believe it—that is their responsibility. Christ does it—that is his part in the conversion of the individual."

Let us linger in the evangelistic atmosphere of those first-century Christians a little longer. As we do, we note that all of the twelve apostles became evangelists except one. That one was Judas who became a traitor. Also, all twelve apostles upon their death were buried in foreign soil except one. That exception was Judas. He was the only one to be buried in his own home country—Judea. The others went far and did much to make Christ known, loved, and obeyed. These early Christians started out with twelve; then there were seventy; then 120, and on Pentecost the number went up to 3,000 followers of Christ. It is estimated that at the end of the first century there were 500,000 followers of Christ; at the end of the second century, 2,000,000; and at the end of the third century, 5,000,000. The whole Roman Empire, by the end of the third century, was honeycombed with the gospel. Christians were found in the hovels of slaves and in the households of the Caesars.

Since these early Christians were able to evangelize so rapidly in spite of adversities and adversaries, what can Christ rightly expect of Christians who live in the twentieth century? Since they were able to do what they did with their limited means of transportation and communication, what might they have done if they had possessed our modern means of communication and transportation? What if they had possessed our modern trains that travel on ribbons of steel? What if they had had access to the modern ocean liners which we have now? What if they had had the airplane by means of which they could have traveled rapidly from one city to another and from one country to another? Also, one cannot help but wonder how far they might have gone in preaching the everlasting evangel if they had possessed our modern printing presses, our telephones, our radios, and our televisions. What if they had possessed our wealth with which to help evangelize their world? For the most part, the early Christians were poor. Perhaps the things we have, they lacked—namely, numbers, modern methods of transportation, communication, and wealth. But perhaps the things they had, we lack—namely, a deep passion and a burning concern to make Christ known to everyone everywhere.

The Need of America—If this were the only compulsion to evangelize, it would be sufficient to keep the churches at the work of evangelism. Jesus shed tears twice—once over a dead man, Lazarus, and again over a dead city, Jerusalem. One day he stood on a hill overlooking Jerusalem.   When he looked at his city, he *saw* its need and cried out, "O Jerusalem, Jerusalem, killing the prophets and stoning those who are sent to you! How often would I have gathered your children together as a hen gathers her brood under her wings, and you would not! Behold, your house is forsaken."   (Luke 13:34.)   Jesus shed tears on that day not because his city lacked fine streets, tall buildings, large parks, and great wealth.   He cried because of his city's need for God.   Religion was formal.   The temple of God was being desecrated and the city was facing destruction.

Try this evangelistic experiment—climb to the top of some hill or mountain or go to the top of some high building and look at your community through the eyes of Christ.   Try to imagine the need of children and youth for him and his teachings.   Try to visualize adults in offices, shops, stores, and on farms, and think of their needs.   Then lift up your eyes and look across the nation and think of its needs of Christ, the gospel message, and the fellowship of the church.   This is an exercise that will help any Christian recapture the evangelistic glow and passion for the redemption of his country.   The unevangelized part of our American population in 1955 was 68,000,000. Millions live daily without knowing Christ and the joy of fellowship with him and the church.

America's greatest need is not more material prosperity, larger banks, taller buildings, more gadgets, more affluence, or more pleasure.   America's greatest need right now is Christ. While there were over 100,000,000 in the United States in 1955 who belonged to some communion, yet there were 68,000,000 who were yet to be evangelized and brought into the fellowship of some church.   Put this 68,000,000 unreached for Christ and the church into a parade.   Start them marching past a given point, six abreast, marching at the rate of sixty steps per minute, eight hours a day. Stand at this given point and watch them go by—this long, seemingly endless line. How long would it be necessary to stand at this given point to watch this parade of boys and girls and men and women pass you? It would take 236 days for this parade to pass by. No one with a real evangelistic concern can look at this long line and not be moved deeply.

Jesus said, "Lift up your eyes, and see how the fields are already white for harvest." (John 4:35.) A part of the problem for many of us is that we look but never see. We look at flowers but never really see them; we look at sunrises and sunsets but never see them. There are those of us who look at people but never really see them. When we look at them, we never really see their need of Christ. The churches of the United States have *the message, the methods,* and *the money* to meet this need. Have they the dedication, passion, and the spiritual power necessary to accomplish this huge task of evangelizing this nation?

The Need of the Church—Well might the church ask the question of the Philippian jailer when he said to Paul, "Men, what must I do to be saved?" The same answer would not be given to the church which was given to the jailer. The reply perhaps would be something like this, "O church of Christ, if you would save yourself, be busy in the salvation of others." The church is always within one generation of extinction. If every church were closed tomorrow; every Bible destroyed; no one ever taught or preached the gospel to anyone else again, and no one ever mentioned the name of Christ to another, the church would go out of existence in one generation. The church lives, grows, and thrives because it evangelizes. When Christians fail to evangelize, the very existence of the church is threatened. Just because the church is here now is no guar-

antee that it will be here 100 or 500 years from now.   If anyone thinks that nothing can happen to the church, let him look
to North Africa where in the early centuries there were many
Christian churches.   They are not there now.   Something has
happened to the churches in Russia.   Their existence has been
and is threatened by atheistic communism.   The life of the
churches in Germany was threatened under Hitler.   Something
can happen to the church on earth.

Something can happen to a local congregation.   Just because it is flourishing in a given community now does not mean
that this will always be so.   Many local congregations have died
which should have lived, because they did not keep at this
business of evangelism.   The church needs evangelism to save
herself from the sterility of a merely cultural religion.   A local
congregation must evangelize or die. Churches will perish unless Christians in every generation seek to evangelize the oncom-
ing generation.   The life of the church and her hope for the
future lie in her reproductive power, which is evangelism.   In
Canada several winters ago, two men were lost in a blinding
snowstorm.   The thermometer was far below zero.   They became numb with the cold.   One of them, more helpless than the
other, finally gave up and lay down in the snow to die.   His
friend did his best to save him.   Though numb with the cold
himself, he began to slap and rub the body of his friend.   He
got him on his feet and walked him about.   It was not long
before the man's body began to warm.   He continued working
until the friend was fully restored.   Suddenly the man realized
that by putting warmth into the body of his companion, he had
put warmth into his own body.   As the church seeks to save
others, she thereby saves herself.   Churches sometimes die but
they never die because they are too evangelistic or too mission-
ary-minded.   Evangelism is not a disease, it is a cure.

Compulsions from Within

"The love of Christ constraineth us." (2 Corinthians 5:14, KJV.) Here is one of the strongest compulsions to evangelism. This word from Paul reveals that which made him an effective evangelist. Love is the greatest compelling force in the world. We speak of "the expulsive power of a new affection." Many men are kept at their daily tasks in factory, shop, store, and on the farm because of their love for wife and children. Many preachers are held to their tasks because the love of Christ constrains them.

John Henry Jowett, once the pastor of the Fifth Avenue Presbyterian Church in New York City, said this about the constraint of Christ's love, "Here is a new constraint. The love of Christ hurries me along like a cloud. I am taken up in its mighty movement and stretched along the appointed road, for it arrests me and makes me its willing prisoner. It lays a strong hand upon me and gives me no option but to go. The man who is the prisoner of the Lord's love will find himself in new and wonderful scenery. Everything will wear a new face—God, man, self, the garden, the sky and trees. We shall look at all things with love's eyes."

The love of Christ constrains us to tell; it compels us to go; it motivates us to give—"that the world might believe." One of the most arresting verses in the New Testament reads, "But God shows his love for us in that while we were yet sinners Christ died for us." (Romans 5:8.) The cross on Calvary speaks its message of deathless love for us.

Whenever you and I look up, we are looking into the face of a Christ who said he would die for us; who not only said it but did it. The test of love is always the length to which it will go. "Greater love has no man than this, that a man lay down his life for his friends." (John 15:13.) There is something here that gets us. Whenever we stand face to face with the cross, we cannot help taking off our hats, and getting down on our knees, and bowing our heads in wonder before the greatness and the graciousness of the love of Christ.

The Love of People—The second compulsion from within is the love of people. There is much today that is likely to make many people cynical and pessimistic about their fellows. When reading is so widespread and when there is a radio or a television in almost every home, we can all know each day what the peoples around the world are doing. We are told so often about the worst in human nature that sometimes we lose confidence in and concern for our fellows. A doctor once said, "I have to watch myself all the time lest I become unsympathetic toward the people I try to heal and help. I am with sickness and suffering so much that I must be on my guard constantly lest my heart become calloused toward the hurts of others." Christ never lost his faith in men even though he knew what was in man. He saw in Simon Peter the rock apostle; he beheld in Andrew, James, and John, tried and true leaders for his kingdom; he saw in Matthew, the tax collector, a faithful and staunch disciple. He saw in Paul a faithful herald of his message.

One of the greatest single needs of our time is the recovery of faith in others. In these days the airwaves are crackling with insinuations and innuendoes. Charges and countercharges are common. The newspapers and magazines are filled with bad news about people. The worst in human nature is played up often on the front page. Under this barrage of bad news, many have become cynical about others, feeling that human nature is human nature and cannot be changed. This leads to a distrust of others.   But human nature *can* be changed.   It has been changed and it is being changed every day through the power of Jesus Christ and his gospel.   When one looks at others through the eyes of Christ, they appear different.   With Vachel Lindsay we can say—

> This is our faith tremendous,
> Our wild hope, who shall scorn,
> That in the name of Jesus
> The world shall be reborn![1]

I Am Debtor—Here is one of the mightiest of all compulsions.   This is the way Paul put it, "I am under obligation both to Greeks and to barbarians, both to the wise and to the foolish."   (Romans 1:14.)   Note that Paul names his creditors— the Greeks, the barbarians; the wise and the foolish.   To know Christ and experience his great salvation will put anyone in debt. Paul did not repudiate his debt.   He started out immediately after his conversion to pay it personally.   He went to Athens to pay his debt to the Greeks but they refused to respond to his message.   He journeyed to Lystra to pay his debt, but they stoned him and left him for dead.   Someone has said, "If Paul had been wealthy he would have become a philanthropist, but since he was poor he capitalized himself and became a pastor-evangelist."   A redeemed life to Paul was a trust, and this attitude toward life will put anyone in debt.

Finding Christ put Andrew in debt.   Immediately he started out to pay his debt by finding his brother, Simon Peter.   On Pentecost, Simon Peter sought to discharge his debt by witnessing for Christ through his sermon on that day.   Meeting and knowing Christ put Philip in debt.   He found Nathanael.   Finding Christ at Jacob's well, put the woman of Samaria in debt.

---

[1] "Foreign Missions in Battle Array," from *Collected Poems* by Vachel Lindsay.   The Macmillan Company.   Used by permission.

She turned immediately and went into her city, saying to her friends, "Come, see a man who told me all that I ever did. Can this be the Christ?" (John 4:29.) What was the result? Many Samaritans in that city believed in him because of the woman's testimony, "He told me all that I ever did." So it is with twentieth-century Christians. We have a debt to pay to those who do not know the Christ we know. Because someone found us, we must find others. Because someone told us, we must tell others.

Harry Lauder, the Scottish comedian, tells the story of an old lamplighter who came before his Scottish home each night to light an old gas lamp. He lifted his lighted stick up into the gas lamp and lit it. After lighting the lamp, the old man zig-zagged his way down the street lighting other lamps. In the deepening twilight, Mr. Lauder soon lost sight of the old man. He said this of him, "I knew where he was all the time by the avenue of light he left behind him." We are lamplighters. We are under compulsion to pass on to others the light we have received.

Henry Crocker wrote a stirring poem entitled "Evangelize" which is a clarion call to all Christians to engage in the primary business of the church—

> Give us a watchword for the hour,
> A thrilling word, a word of power;
> A battlecry, a flaming breath
> That calls to conquest or to death;
> A word to arouse the church from rest,
> To heed her Master's high behest.
> The call is given, Ye hosts arise,
> Our watchword is Evangelize!
> The glad evangel now proclaim
> Through all the earth in Jesus' name.

His word is ringing through the skies,
Evangelize!   Evangelize!
To dying man, a fallen race,
Make known the gift of gospel grace;
The world that now in darkness lies,
Evangelize!   Evangelize!

CHAPTER 2

THE EVANGELISTIC MESSAGE

The word "evangel" means "good news." It is good news about God, for "God so loved the world that he gave his only Son, that whoever believes in him should not perish but have eternal life." (John 3:16.) It is good news, for "God was in Christ reconciling the world to himself." (2 Corinthians 5:19.) It is good news for "In this is love, not that we loved God but that he loved us and sent his Son to be the expiation for our sins." (1 John 4:10.)

The gospel is good news about something that God did in history and something he became in history, in Jesus Christ. The Gospel of John makes this significant statement, "In the beginning was the Word, and the Word was with God, and the Word was God. He was in the beginning with God; all things were made through him, and without him was not anything made that was made. . . . And the Word became flesh and dwelt among us." (John 1:1-3, 14.) The Christian evangel is the good news about the mighty acts of God in behalf of man, whereby God in Christ entered into the human struggle in history; created human perfection; made atonement for sin; conquered death in the risen Christ; and established a new community—a colony of heaven—the Christian church—by his Holy Spirit.

Paul the Apostle said of this evangel we are called upon to teach and preach, "I am not ashamed of the gospel; it is the power of God for salvation to every one who has faith, to the

Jew first and also to the Greek.   For in it the righteousness of
God is revealed through faith for faith; as it is written, 'He who
through faith is righteous shall live.' "   (Romans 1:16-17.)

In 1928 the Jerusalem Conference stated this, "Our message
is Jesus Christ.   He is the revelation of what God is and of
what man through Him may become."   In other words, the
evangel became incarnate in him.   He put a human face on
God.   He perfectly mirrored God, for this gospel of power, redemption, and love in behalf of man was first in the heart of
God.   The evangel was spelled out in Jesus Christ our Lord
for when we want to know what God thinks, we find out what
Christ thinks.   When we want to know how God loves, we find
out how Christ loves.

Paul, the untiring, courageous evangelist, says, "We preach
Christ."   He was Paul's gospel, for Paul's undying theme was
Christ.   His whole horizon was filled with Christ.   He possessed a high Christology.   He never reduced the perfect character, the incomparable teachings or the redemptive work of
Jesus Christ his Lord.   Ultimate loyalty for a Christian is, after
all, not to abstract truth, but it is rather a loyalty to the crucified
and risen Lord Jesus Christ.

D. T. Niles of Ceylon states this in his book, *That They May
Have Life*,[1] "No understanding of Christian evangelism is possible without an appreciation of this nature of the Christian
proclamation.   It is not an affirmation of ideals which men must
test and practice, it is not an explanation of life and its problems
about which men may argue and with which in some form they
must agree; it is rather the announcement of an event with
which men must reckon.   'God has made him both Lord and
Christ.'   There is a finality about that pronouncement.   It
is independent of human opinion and human choice."

---

[1]*That They May Have Life*, by D. T. Niles.   Copyright by Harper & Brothers and
used by permission.

THE EVANGELISTIC MESSAGE 29

While this evangel is good news about God, it is bad news about man. Man is a sinner and needs a savior, "since all have sinned and fall short of the glory of God." (Romans 3:23.) Man never has had, nor does he now have, sufficient resident forces and resources within himself to save himself. Thinking sometimes that he can save himself he becomes a secularist, who tries to live as if there were no God. No thoughtful theologian or preacher today thinks of man—modern man—as being on an escalator going up to new heights under his own power. We do well to remember that it takes more than six inches of earth to grow a Shasta daisy. It takes the help of another world— a summer's sun, rain from the clouds and atmosphere.

However, this fact needs to be stressed also—that while the evangel is bad news about man, it is good news *for* man. It is the best news he has ever heard. Since Christ has come into the world and his message has been proclaimed, men have been different.

The Second Assembly of the World Council of Churches, held at Evanston said this:

> We were hopeless about life and our place in it; He has given us hope and filled our life with meaning. We were hopeless in our sin, unable to do the right; Christ has given us hope. We were hopeless in our suffering and distress; we have seen our affliction turned into blessing by His grace and used for the furtherance of His glory. We were hopeless about the fine outcome of the human story, in distress about the futility of our own efforts; Christ has given us hope. We were hopeless in face of death, trembling between the fear of annihilation and the fear of future punishment, but Christ having overcome the sharpness of death has opened to us the gates of the Kingdom.

This *is* Good News for any man in any and every generation and in all parts of the world.

We are called upon today to preach and to teach this evangel in a time of turbulence and change in our present world. The rapid changes through which we have been passing since the close of World War I in 1918 have been catastrophic. These brief years—less than 50—have been years of cosmic upheavals and a radical disarrangement of our world. We have been and are now living each day in the midst of strain and tension. Since 1914 we have experienced two world wars, a third war in Korea, a fourth war in Indo-China, and a fifth in Egypt. In less than half a century, the world has experienced a Russian revolution; the rise and decline of Fascism; the elimination of Germany and Japan as first-class powers; the fall of France; the independence of India; immense changes in the status of the British Empire; the overthrow of the Chinese Nationalist Government by Communism; the disintegration of the League of Nations; the explosion of the first A-bomb over Hiroshima; and the organization of the United Nations. In the area of religion, there have been the organization of the World Council of Churches in 1948, and of the National Council of Churches of Christ in the United States of America in December, 1950. These recent years have been times also of widespread famine and many concentration camps; dislocation of entire populations; refugees by the tens of thousands; unexpected terror and violence in many nations; millions of men, women, and children killed in war, with this and future generations left with a staggering indebtedness. All this and much more has rocked our humanity violently. No, these recent years have not been years of well-watered gardens, tranquil nights, and cloudless skies. We have been and we are now passing through one of the stormiest latitudes of all history. Some are saying that we may be headed even now into a new Dark Ages.

One thing among many others which characterized the preaching of the prophets in the Old Testament was this—that no matter how dark the future they painted of their day and time, they did not lay down their brushes until they had rimmed the horizon of their dark picture with gold. So it is today, when our modern-day prophets proclaim the evangel, they need to present Christ, the hope of the world.

Whatever else the content of the evangel may be, at least it contains these three facts about the nature, life, and mission of our Lord Jesus Christ—his incarnation, crucifixion, and resurrection. These three incontrovertible facts are remembered annually by Christians in special ways at Christmas, on Good Friday, and at Easter.

Concerning the incarnation, the Fourth Gospel declares, "In the Beginning was the Word, and the Word was with God, and the Word was God. . . . And the Word became flesh and dwelt among us, full of grace and truth; we have beheld his glory, glory as of the only Son from the Father." (John 1:1, 14.) How simply and yet how beautifully Luke describes the coming of the Christchild into the world at Bethlehem, Mary ". . . gave birth to her first-born son and wrapped him in swaddling cloths, and laid him in a manger, because there was no place for them in the inn. And in that region there were shepherds out in the field, keeping watch over their flock by night. And the angel of the Lord appeared to them, and the glory of the Lord shone around them, and they were filled with fear. And the angel said to them, 'Be not afraid; for behold, I bring you good news of a great joy which will come to all the people; for to you is born this day in the city of David a Savior, who is Christ the Lord. And this will be a sign for you: you will find a babe wrapped in swaddling cloths and lying in a manger.' And suddenly there was with the angel a multitude of the heavenly host praising God and saying,

> 'Glory to God in the highest,
> and on earth peace among men with whom he is
> pleased!' " (Luke 2:7-14.)

The Christian evangel begins with the fact of the incarnation. Jesus Christ did not visit this earth of ours by chance for "when the fullness of time was come God sent forth his son." The sending implied a mission. The incarnation was a mission of redeeming love.

David H. C. Read, former Chaplain of Edinburgh University, and at present the pastor of the Madison Avenue Presbyterian Church, New York City, says this about the incarnation,

> That God can be known, and known as our God and Savior, depends for us finally on the fact of Christ. This is above all else what we have to make known to men, "God was in Christ reconciling the world unto himself . . . and entrusting to us the message of reconciliation" (2 Corinthians 5:19). Before we can preach, before we can communicate anything at all to our generation, this is the fact that has to lay hold of us, the one central miracle on which our hope depends—that the Almighty God, in order to bring men and women into a personal harmony with himself and with one another, took our nature and exposed himself to the entire range of human experience, meeting evil in all its forms and accepting the utmost it could do. "The word was made flesh and dwelt among us." In a human body like ours, he was involved in this world. If the church is involved today, it is because she is still his body. He was flesh and blood like us. Our Gospel

is not based upon an idea, an inspiration or a blessed thought. It is based on something far more lasting and solid. The incarnation is an historical event in space and time, that conveys to us and to all who will hear, the assurance of the Living God who forgives and restores and empowers.[2]

The second fact of the evangel is the crucifixion of Christ on Calvary. Here we come face to face with the atonement. There is a cross at the center of the Christian message. Jesus said, "I, when I am lifted up from the earth, will draw all men to myself." (John 12:32.) This cross reveals the sins of men and it also reveals the unwearying love of God. Paul declares, "The word of the cross is folly to those who are perishing, but to us who are being saved it is the power of God." (1 Corinthians 1:18.)

On Calvary's hill there were three crosses. On one cross died a man in his sin. On the opposite cross died a man to sin, and on the center cross died a man for sin. The leaves on one of these trees were blighted. The leaves on the opposite tree were late in coming to their fruition, but the leaves on the center tree were for the healing of the nations. The center cross has deep and far-reaching meanings for every person in every generation. It gets its meaning from the life of Him who hung upon it. He was no stranger to it, for his was an eternal attitude toward it. The cross was not a detached episode in his life, for he was always giving up and giving out. People asked him for bread and he gave them that. They asked him for truth and he gave them that. They asked him for health and he gave them that. Finally, they asked him for his life and he gave them that.

[2]Used by permission of the author.

Did you ever think of the tremendous dimensions of the cross of Christ? How long is it? It is as long as life and time and eternity. How broad is it? It is as broad as the human race. It includes every person. How deep down does it go? It goes down to the deepest sorrow, suffering and sin. How high is it? It is as high as man's holiest thought. It reaches up to the throne of God. Contemplating the meaning of the cross, the Apostle to the Gentiles could say, He "loved me and gave himself for me." (Galatians 2:20.) This makes the cross personal.

In order that men might never forget the cross on Calvary and the one who gave his life upon it, the Lord's Supper was given to the church. The Apostle Paul describes the institution and the purpose of the Holy Communion in this way:

> For I received from the Lord what I also delivered to you, that the Lord Jesus on the night when he was betrayed took bread, and when he had given thanks, he broke it, and said, "This is my body which is for you. Do this in remembrance of me." In the same way also the cup, after supper, saying, "This cup is the new covenant in my blood. Do this, as often as you drink it, in remembrance of me." For as often as you eat this bread and drink the cup, you proclaim the Lord's death until he comes. (1 Corinthians 11:23-26.)

No one wants to be forgotten. Our Lord wanted to be remembered. He fashioned his own monument. Whenever the Lord's table is spread, with the bread and the cup upon it, Christians remember with grateful hearts all that Christ has done for their redemption.

The cross is a signpost to every person. It points the way for him to take on the road of life from the cradle to the grave. In Great Britain, after the battle of Dunkirk, in World War II, the signs at the crossroads were taken down.   Fearing an invasion from the enemy by parachute, they removed the signs to confuse them.   But the people of Great Britain became confused, and many lost their way because the familiar sentinels were down at the crossroads.   Today the human signposts are down along the world's highways.   But there is a sure and dependable signpost along the way of life—it is the cross.   It marks the highway of life for everyone who would find salvation, which comes through the cross.

The third fact of the evangel is the resurrection of Christ. The preachers of the New Testament never pointed men to the cross without showing them the resurrection light breaking behind it.   Like Paul, they decided to know nothing . . . except Jesus Christ and him crucified.   What gave their preaching converting power was the testimony, implicit in every word, that this same Jesus was alive and present and at work in the world.

James S. Stewart of Edinburgh states:

> [The resurrection of Christ] was the tremendous truth that coloured and conditioned all their thinking.   It did not merely give a distinctive accent to their preaching; it throbbed through every word they said.   How could it be otherwise?   Christ risen and alive was for them the one dominating reality of life and the very centre of the universe.   Paul might have put things even more strongly than he did to the Corinthians, "If Christ be not risen, . . . then is our preaching vain?"   He might have added that without the Resurrection, the voice of the [herald of the evangel] would never have been heard in the land.   There was no Christian congregation in that early age which did not recognize itself to be a community of the Resurrection: and there is no

hope of revival in the Churches today until that basic, glorious truth is reasserted and comes back into its own. Far too often we have been inclined to regard the Resurrection as an epilogue to the Gospel, an addendum to the scheme of salvation, a codicil to the divine will and testament. . . . [The resurrection of Christ from the dead] is no appendix to the faith. This *is* the faith. . . . The Lord is risen indeed![3]

The resurrection of Christ from the grave is one of the most incontrovertible facts of history. Overwhelming evidence is provided to us that he arose on that first Easter morning. He appeared eleven different times from the day of his resurrection to the day of his ascension which was forty days. Over 600 persons saw him in his various appearances and believed. The disciples not only believed, they witnessed boldly to the fact of the resurrection. They preached a risen Christ. The church is built over an empty tomb for, "If Christ has not been raised, then our preaching is in vain and your faith is in vain. . . . If Christ has not been raised, your faith is futile and you are still in your sins." (1 Corinthians 15:14, 17.)

These three facts—the incarnation, the crucifixion, and the resurrection of Jesus Christ our Lord—comprise the hard core of the evangelistic message. Here is the foundation of our Christian faith, the preaching and teaching of which produces saving faith, for "Faith comes by hearing and hearing by the word of God." Men do not get a saving faith out of the air. It is mediated to them out of a message and that message is the Christian gospel. Saving faith is not inherited. Each and every person must believe for himself—no one else can believe for him. Therefore it is imperative that the Christian message be presented by every possible means to every person.

---

[3]From *Heralds of God*, by James Stewart. Used by permission of Charles Scribner's Sons, publishers.

The evangelistic message needs to be presented with conviction, if others are to be persuaded to make a decision for Christ to become his disciples and members of the church. The one who communicates the gospel must believe it sincerely him-himself.

The writer is persuaded that pastors do not give the public invitation often enough in order to give those who desire to become disciples of Christ and members of the church an opportunity to do so. Impression without expression is harmful. No pastor when preaching from his pulpit really knows who may be in his audience "almost persuaded" to become a Christian. One Presbyterian pastor I know says something like this in his worship service either before, during, or following his sermon, "If there is anyone here today who would like to talk with me about membership in the church, please see me after the benediction. I will be glad to make an appointment with you to discuss this important matter."

There are a number of pastors in different communions today who give a public invitation to accept Christ at every worship service. This is done by them in the closing part of the sermon as they lead up to and into an invitation hymn.

The writer belongs to a communion—Disciples of Christ—which places special emphasis upon the public invitation as a part of the worship in every morning and evening service. This has been the procedure followed by every pastor during the entire history of this communion since its beginning in 1809. Sometimes no one responds to the invitation during the singing of the hymn, but more often there are those who do. The significant thing about all this is that an opportunity has been given for anyone to respond who loves Christ, has faith in him, and desires to obey him and live a Christian life.

The early ministers of Disciples of Christ presented the gospel of Christ to those not members of any church in three divisions—

facts to be believed; *commands* to be obeyed; and *promises* to be enjoyed.   The facts to be believed were the incarnation, crucifixion, and resurrection of Christ.   The commands to be obeyed were faith, repentance, and baptism.   The promises to be enjoyed were forgiveness of sin, the gift of the Holy Spirit, and eternal life.   This simple division and presentation of the gospel was helpful to many who needed to understand the meaning of the gospel by means of a simple outline that could be easily grasped and remembered.

In the book, *Toward the Conversion of England,* the Anglican Church said, "The aim of evangelism is conversion."   Conversion is produced by obedience to the gospel of Christ.   Conversion is the soul's personal encounter with Him who came to seek and to save that which was lost.   It is produced through belief in and obedience to the Christian gospel.   After conversion comes growth "in the grace and knowledge of our Lord and Savior Jesus Christ."   (2 Peter 3:18.)   After conversion the new Christian can say, "To me to live is Christ."

A small boy one Sunday morning was annoying his father who was reading the Sunday newspaper.   In order to get rid of the boy for a little while, he tore out of the paper a page which had a picture of the world on it.   He tore the page into bits and told his son to go sit down on the floor and put the world together.   The boy returned to his father sooner than expected, saying, "Dad, the world is put back together."   The surprised father exclaimed, "How were you able to do it so quickly?"   The boy's reply was, "You see, Dad, on the other side of the page was a picture of Christ and when I got him in place, the world came out all right."   Just so, when people get Christ in his proper place, life has meaning and takes on eternal significance.

CHAPTER 3

THE EVANGELISTIC MESSENGER

The preacher is a herald of the everlasting evangel. It is said that in the past the messengers of a certain king wore three letters across their breasts—H.M.S., which stood for the words, "His Majesty's Service." Their messages were the king's messages. They carried them with dignity, promptness, and courage.

It is a high honor to be the herald of the King of kings and Lord of lords! To bear his message from his throne to his people is a privilege and a responsibility. He who bears the message of his King is on important business. He is never to think of himself as some little subcommitteeman fussing around with trivial matters. Nor is he to think of himself as a bellboy coming into a hotel lobby with inconsequential announcements. Rather, he is the King's spokesman. The evangel he bears is not his, but that of his King who said, "You did not choose me, but I chose *you* and appointed you." (John 15:16.)

There is a glory in this call to be the King's heralds. Isaiah, the prophetic preacher, saw the Lord in the year that King Uzziah died. The Lord's "train filled the temple. Above him stood the seraphim; each one had six wings: with two he covered his face, and with two he covered his feet, and with two he flew. And one called to another and said:

'Holy, holy, holy is the LORD of hosts;
the whole earth is full of his glory.' " (Isaiah 6:1-3.)
A vision of God came with Isaiah's call.

God goes to peculiar and unlikely places for his messengers. He went to the plains and called Elisha. To the sheepfold for Amos. He walked along the seashore and called four fishermen from their nets to become his heralds. He went to the School of Gamaliel in Jerusalem for Paul, to a farm for Barnabas, and to the seat of customs for Matthew. He calls his messengers from every station in life to be his voice. Today, as always, he is still surprising men by his ways of selecting his messengers. He goes to the shoestore for Moody; to the baseball diamond for Billy Sunday; to the cobbler's bench for William Carey; to a little community in Scotland for Robert Moffat; to a university for John R. Mott and Albert Schweitzer.

The heralds of the Christian message today are in a mighty succession of the great hearts of the calling from Jesus until now. Simon Peter, the Pentecost preacher; Paul, the tireless evangelist; St. Francis of Assisi who "married my lady poverty"; Chrysostom, the golden mouth; Luther, the preacher of God's judgments; John Wesley, savior of England and helper of the world; Alexander Campbell, scholarly interpreter of the scriptures and able preacher of the gospel; Dwight L. Moody, herald of the love of God; J. H. Jowett, peerless interpreter of the word; Charles E. Jefferson, unique expositor of the evangel; and George W. Truett, mighty preacher of God's amazing grace.

It is not easy to be the herald of Christ in any day. It has always been serious and exacting work. This present generation of preachers not only face difficult days in which to preach, but they have some of the greatest opportunities for preaching that have ever been presented. This generation needs the gospel, which is the "power of God for salvation to every one who has faith." (Romans 1:16.)

The question before preachers now in this kind of world is this—"What manner of men should we be who are called to voice the evangel of Christ to this generation? What are the basic qualifications we should have for this high calling? What equipment do we need?"

Preparation

Physical Preparation—The preacher's preparation should include his body, mind, and heart. The physical man has an important part to perform in the heralding of the message. God fashioned the body and without it the soul can do nothing on this earth. It is the soul's medium of expression. The herald of God cannot speak his message without his body, and other things being equal the more healthy his body, the more effective his message. In these exacting days physical strength is needed to "endure hardness as a good soldier of Jesus Christ." By our modern ways of living, nerves get on edge, vitality is sapped, and exhaustion is frequent. We live fast. We rush from one appointment to another. It is quite easy to work with mud, brick, and stone. They stay where they are put. It is easy, comparatively speaking, to work with flowers, for having no emotions they do not lose their tempers. But the preacher works with people who have appetites, dispositions, wills, and passions. These get out of order. He who seeks to deal with frustrations, inner tensions, and complexes must be without such things himself. He must not be a problem seeking to solve the problems of others.

Every herald owes it to his ministry to bring to God, the church, and his work, the best possible physical preparation. Habits that will impair his health and reduce his physical strength should be conquered. God's herald needs to give constant care to his body, for he preaches and works through his body. He is not a disembodied spirit.

Preparation of the Mind—No matter how fine the physique, something besides a healthy body is needed in preaching. He who speaks for God must give constant attention to the making of his mind. His memory must be disciplined. His imagination needs to be kept alive. There are two kinds of heralds of God's message—those of thoughts and those of thought. Continuous study and hard thinking must characterize the ministry today if any man would keep up to date, know God, know the Book of books, understand people and know his world. A preacher cannot give out that which he does not have first himself.

The heralds of God's message of redemption need the best mental equipment that this day affords. God has never put a premium on ignorance. The preacher, as well as others, needs to "love God with all his mind." The herald of today should seek to secure the best education and the finest training possible for his work.

The church at her best has always placed a strong emphasis on education and on an educated ministry. We need head culture. Now and then every herald needs to ask himself the question which Charles L. Goodell used to ask of preachers, "Is your culture a load or a lift? With some men the more they know, the less they do—the more culture, the less feeling." Preaching is the unfolding of truth. It is the evolution of an idea. A herald who can take a great idea and, by sheer force of brain power, unfold it until it glows and hangs glorious before the eyes of man and so burns that hard hearts melt and consciences are awakened is a preacher indeed.

The Spiritual Man—The messenger of God must have not only a strong body and a trained mind but a cultured heart.

It is not only how a preacher thinks but also how he feels, which largely determines the success or failure of his ministry. There is a heresy of the heart as well as of the head. The time is here when the measuring tape needs to be put around the heart as well as the intellect of the one who would speak for God. The herald should speak with his heart and from his heart. He needs to work not only on his message but also on himself. Jonathan Edwards once said, "I make it my first business to look after the salvation of my own soul." This reminds us at once of Paul's concern about himself, saying "lest after preaching to others I myself should be disqualified." (1 Corinthians 9:27.) There is an orthodoxy of the head and there is an orthodoxy of the heart. It is possible for the herald of God to lay claim to an orthodoxy of the head, while at the same time he is heterodox in his heart. Sometimes in his heart he is irritable, unkind, unbrotherly, unco-operative, unappreciative, impatient, domineering, insincere, unsympathetic, and dishonest.

The herald's heart must be set afire. The Word of God confronts the preacher again and again with the fact that the divine fires on the altar of his heart will burn low unless he replenishes the flame at the altar of God. Paul, in writing to the Christians in Rome, stated this, "Never flag in zeal, be aglow with the Spirit." (Romans 12:11.)

Perils

There are perils for preachers just as there are for the laity within the churches. Only three will be considered here.

Lost in his Machinery—In these days of a multiplicity of organizations within the churches, the herald needs to be on his guard lest he become a mere tinkerer of machinery. It is quite easy for a preacher to get lost among the belts, pulleys, and wheels of church machinery, unless he is on constant guard.

Organization is important and necessary. It is not the end but only the means to an end. Preachers are sometimes so interested in creating the machinery of the church that they let the fire go out in the boiler.

In many congregations, organizations multiply until the minister and those associated with him often feel that it takes almost all his time and strength to build, repair, and run the machine. A preacher one time tried to install an electric light in his study. There was a dry-cell battery in one corner of this study by means of which a series of bells over the church were rung for the church school classes. He decided that he would attach an electric light to the dry-cell battery. He bought the necessary electrical equipment, completed the wiring and when all was finished he pressed a button—but there was no light. He sent for an electrician who was a member of his church. The man came and looked the situation over and laughingly said, "Well, pastor, you have preached many sermons to me. Let me preach one to you which will be a sermon in one sentence, 'It takes more power to make a light than a noise.' "

Outside Interests—A second peril of the herald of God is to be found in the many calls that come to him from outside interests. There are many civic organizations, lodges, luncheon clubs, and other community groups that call on him frequently for his services. Unless he is very careful concerning these many requests for his services, he will discover that he does not have much time left to give to his study and his congregation. It is right for a preacher to take some responsibility for civic matters in his community but the best of his time and strength should be given to his church. By his ministry to and through his church he can accomplish more in the long run for the betterment of his community than apart from his church.

Sometimes a minister allows himself to be a server of tables. The herald today, of all days, should not forget the word that comes out of the New Testament church: "It is not right that we should give up preaching the word of God to serve tables. Therefore, brethren, pick out from among you seven men of good repute, full of the Spirit and of wisdom, whom we may appoint to this duty. But we will devote ourselves to prayer and to the ministry of the word." (Acts 6:2-4.)

Misplaced Emphasis—A third peril of the preacher today is a misplaced emphasis. He needs continually to check up on himself to see if he has primary things in primary places. Any ministry can become a tragedy if and when secondary things are put in primary places.

A preacher's emphasis determines the character and quality of his work. A misplaced emphasis by the artist changes portraiture into caricature; a misplaced emphasis by the bugler changes attack into a retreat; a misplaced emphasis by the preacher changes the Christian evangel into man's evasion and it is more fatal than many heresies. A preacher can have anything he wants if he will emphasize it long and prayerfully enough, hard enough and tactfully. If he needs and wants a new church building, he can get it if he will keep on emphasizing it. If he wants a missionary church, he can have that, too, if he will emphasize missions strongly enough. If he really wants an evangelistic church with many baptisms annually, he can have this, too, with a proper, sustained emphasis.

Pulpit

The Pulpit an Altar—The herald's pulpit is not his throne. It is his altar. Here he gives himself sacrificially for Christ and the people. This makes for the romance of preaching. No other attitude will get results which really matter.

The spiritual temperature in the pulpit is determined by the temperature in the mind and heart of the preacher.   In a certain Missouri church there is a pulpit.   On one Sunday morning the writer was in this particular church, preaching from this pulpit.   He looked at the side of the pulpit during the service and saw a thermometer hanging there.   There is no more appropriate place in a church for a thermometer than on the pulpit, for when there are sincerity, concern, and enthusiasm (of the right kind) in the pulpit, there is a warm atmosphere pervading the pews.   A good question for every preacher is, "What is the temperature registered by my pulpit thermometer?"

A Movable Pulpit—Every pulpit should be a movable piece of furniture.   The herald (speaking figuratively of course) should take his pulpit out of the church on Monday morning. He should keep it out all week, speaking from behind it to men and women, one by one or in groups.   In other words, from behind his movable pulpit all through the week he gives his personal witness in the community, in the homes, offices, shops, factories, and on the farms.   Like his Lord he seeks men out one at a time and in groups.   The preacher should have his own prospect list containing names of those who should be members of his church.   He should interview men, one by one, seeking to win them to Christ and church membership.   For many preachers it is easier to preach a sermon from behind the pulpit on Sunday than it is to interview persons one at a time throughout the week and try to secure decisions for Christ.   The path from a preacher's study to his Sunday pulpit should never be a straight one, but a circuitous path, leading from the study over rural roads and city streets to give his redemptive witness in behalf of the One who called him "to seek and to save the lost."

The Pulpit Message—Paul said, "We preach Christ." (1 Corinthians 1:23.)   He is the message for today.   Preachers are a group of men called of God to keep the soul of the world alive through the preaching of the timely, deathless message—the evangel of Christ. They bring the glory of the timeless into time. It is the good news of God the Father to man the sinner. This message is not of man's devising. It is from God. It was said of Dante that he was the voice of ten centuries. The herald of today is the voice of almost twenty centuries. Sylvester Horne, speaking of the preachers of history, says, "They and not kings and warriors have been the moulders of history. The sermons of Isaiah, Micah, Paul, and Peter will outlast the pyramids."

The gospel needs dedicated voices that speak out of trained minds and cultured hearts. The prophet Isaiah (58:1) says, "Lift up your voice like a trumpet." A trumpet sends out a clear musical tone. It never screeches or thunders. The prophet here is thinking of the tone that is characteristic of a trumpet. Its tone is positive. The world judges the preacher today not by what he is against, but by what he is for. The need is for affirmative heralds of the evangel. The tone of a trumpet is penetrating; it sets the nerves vibrating; it awakens the mind and stirs the heart. One cannot sleep when trumpets are blowing. It is a moving tone. It moves to action. It is aggressive. This is the tone needed in preaching today—a trumpet tone. On the first Christian Pentecost, Peter "lifted up his voice." Following his penetrating sermon men cried out, "Brethren, what shall we do?" Peter said to them, "Repent, and be baptized every one of you in the name of Jesus Christ for the forgiveness of your sins; and you shall receive the gift of the Holy Spirit." (Acts 2:38.) The apostle on this occasion preached for a verdict and as a result, "those who received his word were baptized, and there were added that day about three thousand souls." (Acts 2:41.)

Preachers need to preach on big themes. Preachers cannot drop the big themes of the gospel and create great saints. They must always preach upon the great texts of the scriptures; the tremendous passages whose vastnesses almost terrify us as we approach them. Yes, preachers must grapple with the big things of the Christian faith, the things about which their people will hear nowhere else. The message of salvation must be presented to men with a view to securing a decision for Christ. Paul said, "We persuade men" and in all his preaching of the evangel, this is what he did in season and out of season.

Bishop Ralph Cushman of the Methodist Church comments about the preacher like this—

I do not ask
That crowds may throng the temple,
   That standing room may be priced;
I only ask that as I voice the message
   They may see Christ!

I do not ask
That men may sound my praises
   Or headlines spread my name abroad;
I only pray that as I voice the message
   Hearts may find God![1]

The seeking note is often absent in the pulpit message. When this seeking note is present in preaching, it is then that the herald becomes an evangelist. Jesus came saying, "The Son of man came to seek and to save the lost." (Luke 19:10.) His entire ministry was a seeking and a saving ministry. He never allowed himself to forget why he came for he was always seeking and he was always saving.

[1]From *Practicing the Presence,* copyright 1936 by Ralph S. Cushman. By permission of Abingdon Press.

Said a minister, "I simply do not have the evangelistic gift." One wonders how much prayer, thought, and energy he put into it. Francis Peabody once said, "Capacity grows out of desire much more often than desire grows out of capacity."

Jesus said, "This gospel of the kingdom will be preached throughout the whole world." (Matthew 24:14.) That was his word for a troubled world. The civilization of his day had a death rattle in its throat. This message of redeeming love was his hope for a lost world. The Christians took the message out. They matched the power of Christ against the powers of the Caesars. They set something living in a decadent age.

Power

Power Through Prayer—Luther one time said, "Prayer and provender hinder no man on his journey." Men who would preach with power must pray. The diary of the Son of God states, "He went up into the hills by himself to pray." (Matthew 14:23.)

At Lake Wales, Florida, is a building called the Singing Tower. It was built by Edward Bok, the publisher, and dedicated by Calvin Coolidge. John Burroughs suggested a sentence for one of the rooms, which reads, "It is so easy to get lost in the world, I come here to find myself." Prayer does much for the herald of the Good News, that he may find and keep his directions. He needs to pray often in order to meet all his responsibilities with poise and to preach the word with power.

Walter Rauschenbusch was a great scholar. His books have done much to change the course of American Christianity. He emphasized the need of applying the gospel to social needs. For ten years he served a little church on the edge of Hell's

Kitchen in New York City. There he labored untiringly to meet the needs of his people—most of them the victims of misfortune. To explain both his personality and power, one must study his prayer life. Once, during a time of great trial and pain, he wrote:

> In the castle of my soul
> Is a little postern gate,
> Whereat, when I enter,
> I am in the presence of God.
> In a moment, in the turning of a thought,
> I am where God is,
> This is a fact.[2]

Power Through the Herald's Passion—One of America's great preachers used to say, "We are the heralds of a passion but we cannot be the herald of a passion we do not feel." Truth never amounts to much unless it is *felt* truth. Luke says of John the Baptist, "he was a burning and a shining lamp." (John 5:35.) He burned to shine. Robert McCheyne of Scotland died at the age of 29, but after only a few years of preaching he had shaken all Scotland with his message. In 1938 the Archbishop of Canterbury, William Temple, addressed a letter to his clergy requesting them to meet with him for a "quiet day" in London. One of the clergy replied, "Your Grace, in my village we do not need a quiet day but an earthquake."

A few years ago in an address at the Harvard tercentenary celebration President Conant quoted as a warning the words of Edward Gibbon in the *Decline and Fall of the Roman Empire,* written about the Greek scholars of tenth-century Constantinople,

> They held in their lifeless hands the riches of their fathers, without inheriting the spirit which had created and improved that sacred patrimony; they read, they praised, they

---

[2]From "The Postern Gate," from *Walter Rauschenbusch,* by Doris Robinson Sharpe, 1942. Used by permission of The Macmillan Company.

compiled, but their languid souls seemed alike incapable of thought and action. . . . A succession of patient disciples became in their turn the dogmatic teachers of the next servile generation.[3]

These are solemn words. Such degeneration has happened over and over again in history. It can happen to a religious communion. It can happen in a local church. It can happen in a family. Heralds of God may well read these words on their knees, "They held in their lifeless hands the riches of their fathers without inheriting their spirit."

Power Through the Holy Spirit—Christ said to the first disciples, "You shall receive power when the Holy Spirit has come upon you." Halford Luccock says, "The Holy Spirit is the present tense of God." He states that this definition is inadequate, but it does picture the truth enshrined in the words, "the Holy Spirit." It affirms that God is here now, active. To believe in the Holy Spirit is to believe in a God not located back in the past or off in the future, but God in the present. On Pentecost they "were filled with the Holy Spirit." This was the secret of their evangelistic success on this one day when the church was born and 3,000 were baptized.

It is quite easy to tell if the herald of God has the Holy Spirit. If he is daily and continually seeking to win men to Christ and the church, he possesses the Holy Spirit, for the Holy Spirit is an evangelistic spirit. Theodore Adams, minister of the First Baptist Church of Richmond, Virginia, was ordained by his preacher father who said in giving the charge to his son, "Ted, my son, keep close to Christ. Ted, my son, keep close to men. Ted, my son, bring Christ and men together." This is the

---

[3]From Chapter LIII.

herald's supreme task—to keep close to Christ and to bring men to Christ for salvation.

Paul said to young Timothy, "Do the work of an evangelist." (2 Timothy 4:5.) This is a timely word from a seasoned veteran to a raw recruit. This word needs to be displayed in every Bible college and in every seminary; carved into every pulpit; placed in every preacher's study and stamped indelibly on the heart of every herald of the Good News.

CHAPTER 4

THE EVANGELISTIC CHURCH

Jesus Christ our Lord never said "my home" for he had none. He never said "my child" for he had none, but he did say, "my Father" and "my church." Of his church he said, "I will build my church and the powers of death shall not prevail against it." (Matthew 16:18.) Christ loved his church with an unspeakable love as indicated by the apostle Paul in his statement, "Christ loved the church and gave himself up for her, that he might sanctify her, having cleansed her by the washing of water with the word, that the church might be presented before him in splendor, without spot or wrinkle or any such thing, that she might be holy and without blemish." (Ephesians 5:25-27.) Christ is the head of the church and the church is his body. The church is both divine and human—divine because Christ is its head and human because you and I and other millions like us belong to and are a part of his body, the church. Christ is also the foundation of his church "For no other foundation can anyone lay than that which is laid, which is Jesus Christ." (1 Corinthians 3:11.)

The Christian church began on the first Pentecost as recorded in Acts, chapter 2. It was born in a revival with amazing evangelistic results. Following Simon Peter's sermon 3,000 were baptized in one day. It was a day of evangelism. The work of preaching the gospel and of soul-saving, begun on the first Christian Pentecost, was continued without ceasing in those early days for "the Lord added to their number day by day those who were being saved." (Acts 2:47.) Pentecost cannot be duplicated but it can be perpetuated and its spirit captured. One thing among many others that happened on the first Christian Pentecost, which can be perpetuated, is its evangelism.

The Book of Acts is the greatest book on evangelism ever written. It tells of many conversions; the organization of new churches and of aggressive evangelistic work throughout the Roman Empire. It is said of the New Testament fellowship of believers, "The church throughout all Judea and Galilee and Samaria had peace and was built up; and walking in the fear of the Lord and in the comfort of the Holy Spirit, it was multiplied." (Acts 9:31.) The church of that day was a converting agency.

The evangelistic passion which was at the heart of the New Testament church is needed in the life and work of the modern twentieth-century church. That there is much lethargy, unconcern, and indifference about evangelism in many congregations of our day and time, throughout America, is indicated again and again by the large number of congregations in all communions which did not have even one baptism last year. In 1955 in New York City, which has a population of over 8,000,000, one well-known Protestant communion with sixty-four congregations reported that thirty-eight of these had an increase of one or more new members. Twenty-two had a decrease in membership and four marked time. The membership of the sixty-four churches is 30,543. The net increase in membership for an entire year was 52. At this rate, how long will it take to evangelize the more than 4,000,000 people in New York City who are still unreached by any religious body—Jewish, Roman Catholic, or Protestant?

One Protestant communion in one of the large states in America reported that for 1955 its 554 churches, with a resident membership of 103,985, had 4,142 baptisms. This means that it took 25 members one entire year to win and baptize one person. Only seven of the 554 churches had 50 or more baptisms. In another state during 1955, in this same Protestant communion, it took 52 members one entire year to win and baptize one person. Now and then someone is heard to say, "I don't believe in numbers" and another is heard to say, "I'm afraid of numbers in evangelism." At the slow rate that some of our Protestant churches are evangelizing today, no one anywhere needs to be unduly alarmed about numbers. Facts are that in most places there are no numbers to be alarmed about. The concern today should be with reference to the terrible lack of numbers in our evangelism. Some congregations are doing well in their evangelism but others have forgotten the command of Christ to "go make disciples." What must Christ think of a congregation, with a full-time minister, a good building, a church school with children, young people and adults enrolled, and located in a community with a number of unchurched people in it and yet reporting no new members in one whole year? In such cases, churches have lost the zeal and passion to win others to Christ. The command of Christ has become an elective instead of an imperative.

Some churches belong to the cult of the comfortable. They have become satisfied with themselves. They are neglecting their outreach responsibility. A minister and his congregation built a new building on a busy, noisy street corner in a large city. In order to shut out the noise, the minister requested the architect to draw plans for huge doors, through which people came into the church sanctuary from the street. After the building was completed the minister took a friend of his from the street through the huge, thick doors. The minister shut the doors tightly, then turning to his friend said, "Listen, you can't hear a thing on the outside, can you?" It is tragic and even sinful, when any congregation anywhere cannot hear a thing on the outside. Evangelism keeps the ears of a congregation sensitive to the needs of those outside its fellowship.

Jesus said to four fishermen who were standing on the shore of the Lake of Galilee and who had been out all night and caught nothing, "Put out into the deep and let down your nets for a catch." (Luke 5:4.) Shorelines are overfished. The call of Christ is to launch out into deep water. We are told that the people of the Federated Malay States fish in rice furrows, catching small fish, while before them, in full view, the great ocean rolls.

The Protestant churches of our nation may well consider their present and future evangelistic opportunities and responsibilities. These are staggering. America is changing in population. The total population of the United States was 168,000,000 as of July 1, 1956, according to the United States Census Bureau. The population is increasing at the rate of about 7,500 daily. It is estimated that by 1975 the population will have increased from 168,000,000 to 220,000,000. This means that in twenty years 52,000,000 more persons will be living in the United States than are here now. This increase of 52,000,000 is equal to the entire population west of the Mississippi River, with all of New England added.

The entire population map of the nation will be changed radically in the next twenty years. Many wide-open spaces will be occupied; new centers of population will be formed; new markets will be created; enlarged transportation systems will be needed; additional educational buildings will be required; and larger and more religious facilities will be necessary.

We are told that every one of the 48 states will share in the increase of population over the next twenty years. Population experts think that California, now the second state in population, will be the largest by 1975 with 26,000,000 people within her borders. The other states that will have the largest percentage of growth during the next 20 years, so they say, are Washington, Oregon, Nevada, Arizona, New Mexico, and Florida. By 1975 Texas, the largest state in area, will have about 3,600,000 more people within her borders than now, which will mean a total population in the state of over 12,000,000. By that time the Lone-Star State will be a rival of Illinois for fifth place.

At present, there are fewer persons in the United States without affiliation with some religious denomination, in relation to the total population, than at any time in the nation's history. The largest number of unchurched was reported in 1940 when the figure rose to 67,200,000 in a population of 132,122,000. By 1954 the number of unchurched had declined to 64,200,000 out of a population listed as 161,762,000. The latest figure on church membership in the nation as given for 1955 is 100,162,529. This is the total membership of all faiths. This means that 60.9% of the nation now belongs to some denomination and is so counted and reported in the membership statistics by the denominations. This 60.9% is the highest percentage of the nation's population ever reported as belonging to some religious group or denomination.

Of the 100,162,529 members of some religious body in the United States, 5,500,000 are Jewish; 33,396,647 are Roman Catholic, and 58,446,567 are Protestant. Other and smaller church bodies make up the remainder of the church membership figures.

Some religious bodies count their church members differently. Only two or three Protestant bodies count all baptized children when reporting their church membership. Others count only those who are communicant members. Usually communicant or "full members" of the church are those 12 years of age and over. It is very important to note this difference in recording church members, for if the Protestant churches counted all their children up to 12 years of age, as is done by the Roman Catholic Church, their numbers would increase from 58,448,567 to something like 75,000,000. On the other hand, if the Roman Catholic Church counted its members as do the Protestant churches, then instead of reporting 33,396,647 they would report only about 20,000,000.

This increase has been going on year after year for the past 30 years. In 1926 the membership of all churches in the United States was 54,000,000; in 1936 there were 55,000,000; in 1946 there were 73,000,000; and in 1956 there were over 100,000,000. The net increase in church membership in 30 years has been 96% while the population of the nation during the same 30 years increased 31%. Percentagewise, the increase in church membership has been as follows—in the year 1800, 6% of the population belonged to some church; 1850—16%; 1900— 36%; 1950—53%; and 1955—60%.

This increase is not primarily because of the fear of the A-bombs or the H-bombs. Nor is it because of a sense of uncertainty or insecurity on the part of Americans. Nor is it because it is the popular thing to unite with a church. Rather, this steady increase in membership is because the churches during the past 30 years have been working at this big business of evangelism. More money has been spent; more literature has been printed and distributed; more evangelistic books have been written; more laymen and laywomen have been trained for personal evangelism; more teachers have been inspired; more evangelistic meetings have been held; and more pastors have been enlisted in evangelism than ever before in the history of America.

Beginning about 1900 and for a quarter of a century afterward, evangelism was pushed to the edges. It became marginal. Other things became central. At present evangelism is primary and central in the life and work of most congregations and denominations. So long as the churches keep New Testament evangelism central, all will go well. It is when churches are most evangelistic and most missionary that they write their most glorious history.

To care for the present church membership it is reported that there are 280,000 church edifices in the nation. Of that number, 15,600 are Roman Catholic, 3,400 Jewish, and 261,000 Protestant. This number of buildings is totally inadequate to care for the increasing population. Our nation is not only changing in population but it is changing in character. It is rapidly becoming urbanized. In 1870, 40% of the population lived in cities and 60% lived in rural areas. At present, 65% of the nation's population live in urban centers, while 35% reside in the rural areas. This means that the new evangelistic frontier is in the cities. It is estimated that at least 70,000 new suburban churches will be needed in the next twenty years as a result of these rapid population shifts. It is further estimated that the suburban population, now at 45,100,000, will reach 83,400,000 by 1975. Thus, the implications for evangelism are far reaching. This tremendous growth is a summons to a larger evangelism on the part of every denomination. Also, to care for the increase in population in all 48 states from 1950 to 1975 will require around 100,000 additional church buildings and

75,000 more ministers. All this calls for wise kingdom states-manship and a sense of urgency.

At the same time, when new congregations are being organ-ized and more new buildings are being erected, more young men and women must be found and trained in the Bible colleges and seminaries of the nation, for full-time Christian service.

There has never been a time in the history of the churches of America when there were as many young men and women in our Bible colleges and seminaries as now. This is encouraging. But more are needed. Also, more buildings are an urgent ne-cessity. More gifts and larger endowments are required if the churches are to be adequately supplied with trained and dedi-cated ministers for the evangelization of America.

All those who are interested in the evangelistic progress of the churches are concerned that each Bible college and seminary shall have definite instruction as a part of the curriculum with reference to evangelism. Instruction in evangelism should not be tucked away in a corner somewhere or relegated to a secondary place in seminary courses. A survey conducted several years ago by the Department of Evangelism of the National Council of Churches indicated two things: First, there were those Bible colleges and seminaries that gave definite courses in evangelism. They gave it a dignified place in the curriculum. Then, second, there were others that gave very little instruction in evangelism as to its meaning or the methods by which it is to be carried on. And it was also found that there were few up-to-date books on evangelism in the libraries of the institutions in this second group.

It is next to impossible to have an evangelistic church without an evangelistic minister. With the present-day organization in the Protestant churches, the minister is looked upon as the leader. He, more than anyone else, sets the tone and determines the emphasis of his church. Since this is true, then the churches have a right to expect that their Bible colleges and seminaries will put the evangelistic spirit into the minds and hearts of young ministers and train them to do the work of an evangelist.

Rapid changes and the large increases in population summon the churches to a larger and a more effective evangelism. All this must begin in each Protestant congregation, of which there are 275,000 in the nation. If evangelism does not happen in the local congregation, it does not happen. It must start there or not at all. If something significant is to happen there, then at least four things are necessary:

1. *A warm evangelistic atmosphere.*—One cannot grow seeds in frozen ground. It is impossible to develop American Beauty roses in a refrigerator. It is impossible, also, to have evangelistic results in a church where there is a cold, indifferent, and apathetic attitude toward the winning of others to Christ.

2. *A deep concern for the lost.*—Jesus our Lord said of himself, "The Son of man came to seek and to save the lost." (Luke 19:10.) Every word in this sentence is a monosyllable. The same passion and concern for the lost that was in his heart must also be in the heart of every congregation. A church must never lose this seeking and saving note in its ministry.

3. *The practice of prayer.*—Increasingly churches are forming prayer groups. These groups, composed of ten to fifteen members each, meet weekly. They pray for the minister, the sorrowing, and the sick. They pray for persons on the responsibility list of the congregation whom they desire brought to Christ and into the membership of the church. The pulpit prayers of the ministers in such churches are saturated with evangelistic concern for the unreached of the community. "Prayer changes things" and it can and will change the evangelistic outlook and concern of any congregation.

4. Christians, a channel of power.—Jesus promised the early Christians, "You shall receive power when the Holy Spirit has come upon you." (Acts 1:8.) This promise was fulfilled on Pentecost and afterward. This same promise is for the churches of today. The Holy Spirit was given in order that Christians might be empowered for witnessing in behalf of Christ. He must have an open channel through which to work. The Holy Spirit is an evangelizing spirit. He is concerned for the salvation of men and nations. Some scholars have suggested that the name of the fifth book in our New Testament be changed from "The Acts of the Apostles" to "The Acts of the Holy Spirit."

A Program of Evangelism

A program of evangelism for every congregation is of primary importance and it is essential if there are to be adequate results. An evangelistic program may be seasonal, following the four church calendar seasons of the year—

New Year's to Easter; Easter to Pentecost; Pentecost to World-Wide Communion Sunday; and World-Wide Communion Sunday to Christmas.

A program of evangelism should be at least one year in length for every congregation. Some churches work out a three- or five-year program which has many advantages. A program of evangelism should be large enough to challenge a congregation to do greater and better work. Do you who are older remember the old flat maps that were studied in the public schools? The equator was at the center of the map. The map had two dimensions—length and breadth. The new maps today are different. The north pole is the center and a new dimension, depth, has been added. Our world looks altogether different when presented to us with a new center and an added dimension.

Many churches need to draw new maps. Old maps, former programs, and past goals are not large enough in most churches—not in an atomic era.

What should be included in an evangelistic program for a local congregation whether rural or urban? The following are a few items in the program which are basic and necessary:

Educational Evangelism—The Sunday church school and the daily vacation Bible school are significant evangelistic agencies. The teacher is the key in all these educational processes. If the evangelistic concern is absent in the heart of the teacher, there will be no evangelistic results in her class or department. Five simple steps in educational evangelism are: want them, reach them, teach them, win them, and hold them. What could not the 3,000,000 teachers and officers of our church schools in America do in evangelism if they became more concerned about their evangelistic responsibility? If a boy or girl attends a church school from the Nursery Department through the Intermediate Department and has not become a communicant member of the church in that time, then someone has blundered somewhere. Some teacher or parent has overlooked his or her evangelistic responsibility.

Home Evangelism—The home should be recognized as a vital factor in the evangelistic program of a local congregation. The interest and help of parents should be enlisted in the winning of their children and young people to Christ. There are 46,000,000 homes in America. Of this number some 16,000,000 are not identified with any church. This means that the leaders in each congregation have a double duty. The first is to bring to the attention of all homes identified with the church, a sense of responsibility for the teaching and winning of their own children for Christ.

The second is to try to win all the families of the community which are outside the membership of any church. This is a big order. One local congregation in a Midwestern city was quite successful in reaching unchurched families by the use of a simple method. Twenty-four families of the congregation were made responsible for twenty-four families not connected with any church in the community. Each church family promised to cultivate its assigned family for at least one year through calls, invitations to dinner, literature, invitations to go with them to church and to integrate each member of the family into some organization of the church for acquaintance and fellowship. It worked. Family after family came into the membership of the church through this process of cultivation.

The catechetical or pastor's class—With some congregations this class has been a part of their evangelistic program for years. It is planned for and put into the program annually. Some of these classes continue from four weeks to two years. The tendency among pastors is to lengthen the time for these classes, which is highly commendable. Almost every denomination has produced excellent materials for the use of pastors in preparing children, youth, and adults for church membership. The pastor usually is the person who teaches this class. If he finds it impossible to do this, then some other qualified person should be made responsible for this task. These classes are usually conducted after school, on Saturdays, or on Sunday mornings. The instruction in preparation for church membership should be thought of as being supplemental to the teaching by the church school teachers, and not as a substitute for their teaching.

The responsibility list—The gathering of a responsibility list and its cultivation is not easy but it is absolutely essential for evangelistic success. This subject is discussed in the chapter on "Evangelism of Adults."

Visitation Evangelism—A group of laymen and laywomen should be carefully selected, trained, and used for interviewing those on the responsibility list with the definite purpose of securing a decision for Christ and the church. This should be done once each year in every church, rural or urban, and in many churches twice annually. Definite dates should be set, literature ordered, and workers trained. This plan is discussed in the chapter, "Evangelism of Adults."

Preaching Missions—More preaching missions (evangelistic meetings) are being held today by more churches than ever before. These are held for periods of eight days to four weeks in length with the pastor of the local congregation or a guest minister doing the preaching night by night. There is still a big need for such missions. If they are to succeed in attendance, if new members are to be added to the church, if the moral tone of the community is to be lifted, and if the local congregation is to be awakened spiritually, then there must be adequate preparation from six months to one year prior to the mission. Interdenominational preaching missions will be discussed in a later chapter of this book, hence will not be considered here.

There are other methods which a congregation may use in its evangelism but the above are considered basic for securing evangelistic results. If a local congregation carries out its evangelistic program, it must organize to do so.

Evangelistic Committee—When a congregation desires to do anything worth while, it appoints some group to be responsible for carrying out its program or some part of it. A committee or a department of evangelism should be appointed to be responsible for giving leadership and direction to the congregation. Those appointed should represent the various organizations within the congregation such as Christian education, youth fellowships, men's fellowship, women's missionary organizations, and so forth. This committee or department of evangelism should organize itself and report on its work from time to time to the board of officers of the church. This committee or department needs to provide itself with evangelistic literature from its denomination. It should consider and decide what should be ordered for distribution to, and study by, the congregation.

One of the most important responsibilities of this group is to formulate a program of evangelism along lines already indicated in this chapter, and then give leadership to it. This should be done with vision, faith, and courage. It is also the responsibility of this group to keep the evangelistic concern and passion in the program of the church; to focus the attention of the church on "the fields that are white unto harvest" and to aid the minister of the church in winning others to Christ.

Membership Days—Any time is a good time to unite with the church. However, there is value in working toward a few special membership days in an annual program of evangelism. In the Lenten season, Palm Sunday or Easter, or both, are excellent days on which to receive a number of new members into the fellowship of the church. Pentecost is another day that can be made a day of special ingathering. World-Wide Communion Sunday, the first Sunday in October, is another day toward which the local congregation can work as a day on which to receive new members. The Advent Season leading up to Christmas can be made a special season for evangelism which may be brought to its climax on Christmas Sunday. Here are four Sundays of the year toward which every congregation can work as special days when new members may be received. Evangelistic success on each day is determined largely by the preparation that is made for these special membership days.

The evangelistic church in a changing America will be concerned today in the organization of new churches. Many more are needed. New housing projects are being multiplied and new communities are springing up. In some places in America there is overchurching, but also there is a vast amount of underchurching in others. The denominations are giving increased attention to their responsibilities in the organization of new churches. In most cases comity is recognized and practiced in the "planting" of new churches.

New Churches Needed

Millions of dollars have been raised within the past ten years and more millions are yet needed to care adequately for the present urgent need for more new congregations and more new buildings. One of the pressing problems for any new congregation which plans to purchase land and build on it is the matter of securing sufficient land for parking facilities. It is estimated that the minimum cost of a new church building or a first unit is $75,000. If 100,000 new buildings are needed between 1950 and 1975, then it will be necessary for the churches to provide $7,500,000,000 for this purpose.

Many large churches are finding deep satisfaction these days in contributing some of their members and funds to help start new congregations in underchurched communities. This is an unselfish thing to do. When a new congregation is organized and a new building is constructed, think what happens after that! Boys and girls are taught the Book of books, the community is provided a place in which to meet together for Christian worship and fellowship, the gospel is preached week after week, people are converted, young people decide for the ministry and other full-time Christian service, dedicated dollars are given for missionary work in the United States and in other lands, and the kingdom of God is extended throughout the whole wide world. The writer has said often that if he had $1,000,000 to give away, he would designate one half of it for the purpose of organizing new congregations in communities where new ones were needed and the other half he would give to seminaries for the training of ministers to become the leaders of these new congregations.

During the last war a severe storm swept the coast of northern England and destroyed the church in one of the villages. The people were poor and felt they could not rebuild their church. They met in the homes of members. One day a British admiral came to the village, looked up the minister, and asked if the congregation planned to rebuild its church. The minister related their plight and said they were not able to rebuild. "Then," said the admiral, "if you cannot rebuild your church, the British government will build it for you. You see, the spire of your church was a landmark to sailors at sea and it is so indicated on all the maps of the British Navy. It would be cheaper for us to rebuild your church than to make new maps." The church must always be a landmark pointing the way to Christ and it must ever be an evangelizing agency in behalf of the lost of all generations.

CHAPTER 5

EVANGELISM OF CHILDREN

The United States has never had so many children under sixteen years of age as it has now. Each year since Pearl Harbor an average of 4,000,000 babies have been born. The year 1956 records the birth of 4,200,000 babies. They are being born at the rate of one every 8 seconds or 35 every five minutes, 458 every hour, or 11,000 new baby citizens every 24 hours. We have a booming baby business in America. It is predicted that by 1965, instead of a 4,000,000 "baby crop," the number of babies will reach 5,000,000 annually.

These babies have rights. They not only have rights to good homes, excellent schools, modern hospitals, sanitary communities, sufficient food and clothing, but also they have spiritual rights. They have a right to know the Bible; to have the concern and love of the church and to know Jesus Christ as the friend of all children.

Let us look again at the four million babies born annually in America. Many thousands of them will grow up like little pagans, for they have been born into homes where there are no Christian pictures on the walls; no Christian conversation is heard; no grace at meals is said; no Christian literature is read, and no Christian teaching is received. They will grow up in a pagan atmosphere *unless* the churches find them, teach them, and supply the spiritual training which after all is the primary responsibility of a home.

The writer knows of an Oklahoma church which placed special emphasis on its nursery roll. At one time there were 300 babies on its roll. A county committee of fifty women served to look out for babies in order to secure their names, birthdays, and addresses for the nursery roll. These babies were called on by the women, their birthdays remembered, and the fathers and mothers invited to attend the parents' Bible class. The efforts of this committee for a number of years resulted in new scholars for the church school. Many parents united with the church. Surely the time is here when the churches should take more interest and also have a larger concern for the baby-hood of their communities.

There is no part of the church's life and program that is more important than that which has to do with the children. Pay attention to the children. The hand that opens the door of a home wider and more quickly than any other hand is the dimpled hand of a baby. If a church has time for the baby of a home, that home usually has time for the church.

The word of yesterday was *rescue* but the divine whisper of today is *prevent*. The greatest doctor in the community is not the doctor who cures disease, but the doctor who prevents dis-ease. The greatest statesman in the kingdom of God is the one who prevents growing boys and girls from going to the prodigal son's territory.

Several years ago in Long Beach, California, there lived a family that had the misfortune to lose a Boston Bull terrier. They advertised in many papers; searched in five states for three months; spent their savings and mortgaged their home— all for the sake of finding their pet dog. If a family will do all this in order to find a lost dog, what should church school teachers and other church leaders be willing to do in order to find boys and girls who have been allowed to slip out and away from the fellowship and the teaching ministry of the church? Daniel Webster was seen to tip his hat to a boy one afternoon. When asked why, he replied, "I did so when I thought of the wonderful possibilities wrapped up in that little brain and what it could mean for good to his generation."

There is no more important work in America today than that of training the children. Yet the mother in the home is listed in the census as "unemployed." The teacher in the classroom usually is paid less than the worker who built the room. The teaching of the Bible, the basic book for character building, is too often forbidden in the public schools, and neglected in the home. The church school is often understaffed, and volunteers are hard to find. If we are wise, we will spend more time and more money training our children to whom we shall soon relinquish our stores, our factories, our farms, our nation and our churches.

While the Christian education program is not as vigorous and thorough as it should be in order to meet the spiritual needs of our vast numbers of children, yet splendid progress is being made. The 1955 figures show that the church schools are overflowing with a new total of 37,623,530 students and teachers. All but 7% of this grand total are Protestants. This is an increase over the previous year of 2,234,064. Church school teachers and officers, most of them volunteers, now number 2,970,614, or almost 250,000 more than the year before. This number is not sufficient. At least 500,000 more are needed now. While church membership was increasing 2.8% in 1955, the church schools were increasing 5.3%.

In order to meet new needs in Christian education, accentuated by this rapid increase in population, the churches in 1956 raised over $800,000,000 for the construction of new buildings and for the repair and enlargement of old buildings. Even in the light of this encouraging building program, not enough church building is going on to meet the situation caused by the rapid increase in population. Concerning the spiritual nurture of childhood and youth, the churches need to think and plan ahead for the next 20 years. It is predicted that during the ten years from 1955 to 1965, there will be an increase up to a total of 51,502,000 in the elementary schools, high schools, and colleges of America. Every one of the students is a potential church school scholar.

Providing more buildings and teachers is not the only problem America faces with reference to the children. There are many evil and sinister influences at work in America to capture the interest, minds, and hearts of children.

One evil influence is produced for radio and television by the beer and wine advertisers. In 1956 the Public Relations Committee of the United Church Women of Southern California and Southern Nevada conducted a careful survey of television beer and wine commercials during child viewing hours. They made tape recordings substantiating all commercials. To the amazement of the women there were found to be as many as twenty-seven beer and wine commercials per evening, and an average of nineteen an evening while the children watch.

The reason for the frequency of the spot announcements is plain to see. What is not so readily understood is that these "spots" are so placed in relation to highly recommended children's programs (usually sponsored by most acceptable products) as to give respectability to the objectionable. Also, the survey points out how the beer and wine advertising comes jauntily into the homes, disguised in catchy jingles and appealing pictures, to charm the eyes and ears of children from the time the stations open with their pledge to serve the public welfare until they come to their patriotic close at the end of the day.

The following revealing statement appeared in the June 1955 issue of *Brewers Journal:*

> The future looks bright. Soon now, the large group of war and postwar babies will begin reaching legal drinking age and the brewers will have that bigger market for their product; and it will be the best group of beer drinkers to come along in a long while, because more of these people have seen beer served in their home and come to accept it as a perfect social beverage than ever before in history.[1]

It is not legal in most states to sell beer and wine to minors and yet each evening in millions of homes across our land it is being sold to children.

Evangelistic Responsibilities

What does all this increase in the number of children mean to the churches in their evangelism? The responsibility is so staggering that it makes one think and think hard and long. First, there is the outreach responsibility. In every community there are many children not receiving any Christian teaching whatever. How sincerely does a local congregation want more children within its teaching ministry, and how hard is it willing to work to go out into the community to get them?

Second, there is the teaching responsibility. After we reach children, we must teach them. This means good lesson materials, trained and dedicated teachers, and sympathetic pastors. Did you ever ask yourself why the difference in evangelistic results on the first Pentecost and on Mars Hill? Peter was the Pentecost preacher and Paul was the preacher on Mars Hill. On Pentecost there were 3,000 baptized in one day, and on

[1]From *Clipsheet,* September 26, 1955.

Mars Hill only several decided for Christ. What made the difference? Both men were great preachers and both sermons were great messages. The difference in the results was partly this— Peter preached to Jews. His sermon was presented to a people who were intelligent in their Old Testament scriptures. They knew the Old Testament scriptures, having been taught meticulously in their homes and synagogues. They were looking for their Messiah. Paul preached his sermon to the Greeks, who had never heard of the one true God. They were totally ignorant about the God and the Christ Paul was preaching about, hence there were only a few converts. He preached his evangelistic message against a background of total ignorance about God and the scriptures. So it is today—if we want larger and better evangelistic results, we must do more and better Christian teaching in the home and the church.

In an editorial which appeared in *The Christian-Evangelist,* a weekly journal of Disciples of Christ, the editor had this to say about the value of children and our responsibility for their spiritual nurture and training: "The Kimberly diamond mines in South Africa recently turned up one of the largest diamonds ever found. And thereby hangs a parable. The diamond was delivered to a skilled cutter who spent two months at the task of bringing out the stone's fabulous beauty in all its prismatic perfection. Michael Abrahams, the diamond cutter to whom the task was assigned, said he could hardly sleep for thinking of the risk. In fact, no insurance company would cover the risk of the cutting.

" 'One slip and I would have been ruined,' he said. The diamond, originally one hundred carats, was cut to sixty carats for marketing, and in the hands of the skilled workman became a remarkable gem of beauty. Now for the moral. Church school teachers, preachers, and parents who touch the lives of little children are dealing with something far more precious than diamonds found in a Kimberly mine. Do they lose sleep for 'thinking of the risk'? It could well be that 'one slip' and they too may be ruined! Perhaps it was the sensing of this great responsibility of the teacher that caused James to write:

> Let not many of you become teachers, my brethren, for you know that we who teach will be judged with greater strictness. For we all make many mistakes. . . . (James 3:1-2.)

"And yet, as with all parables, this one must not be made to go on all fours. Children are not cold lifeless diamonds, they are more like growing plants that need tending and the sunshine of sympathetic understanding and love. But if a diamond cutter can scarcely sleep for the risk he takes, how much more concern must parents and teachers have who carry the sacred responsibility of precious human lives with their eternal destiny in their hands?"

Third, there is the evangelistic responsibility. This responsibility falls heavily on the teachers. If the minister of a church is expected by the church school teachers to preach for a verdict, then the minister has a right to expect the teachers to teach for a verdict. Most teachers do, but a number go on in their work of teaching from week to week, without any evangelistic concern for the children in their care. If a boy or a girl in the church school is not a member of the church by the time he or she is 15 years of age, someone has failed somewhere. It may be that the teacher, pastor, or the parents have failed to bring children to a conscious acceptance of Jesus Christ. "Those who are wise shall shine like the brightness of the firmament; and those who turn many to righteousness, like the stars forever and ever." (Daniel 12:3.) The church school should be and must be an evangelistic agency.

In May, 1944, the Winning the Children for Christ Program was launched at the American Baptist Convention in Atlantic City by this denomination. A new, daring plan of evangelistic outreach and Christian education was undertaken. For 12 years since 1944, some remarkable results have been achieved. Over 1,500 Baptist churches have conducted the program under supervised, trained leadership; 5,000 Bible story hours have been conducted; over 50,000 children have been reached and the movement has brought over 25,000 children into some church school.

This Winning the Children for Christ Program is sponsored jointly by the Department of Evangelism of the Home Mission Societies and the Board of Education and Publications of the American Baptist Convention. There are four well-trained women on the national staff, who travel among the churches constantly to conduct these programs in behalf of the unreached children of our nation. Here is a method of reaching and interesting children that is most effective. May the day soon come when many other communions will find it possible to use the method initiated by the Baptists.

Conversion of Children

What about the conversion of children? They can have a child's experience in a personal acceptance of Christ. Conversion may be gradual or sudden. It may be like the growing of wheat fields; growth is quiet but nevertheless very real. Or it may be like a thunderstorm when the elements of nature are greatly disturbed by wind and lightning.

A child of 10 to 15 years of age should not be expected to have the conversion experience of a prodigal adult. After careful teaching in the home and the church school, it is natural and normal for a child at the age of 10-15 to make his own personal decision to accept Christ and become a member of the church. The unnatural and abnormal thing would be that after being taught the Bible, he or she would not desire to become a conscious follower of Christ. It is just as natural for boys and girls to turn to Christ when rightly taught as it is for American Beauty roses to turn their faces to the sun. It is normal for children to love the lovely.

Adults need to give children the opportunity to make their Christian decision. This public decision may be anticipated and provided for through personal conferences, through catechetical or pastor's classes, and through well-planned decision days. When children become members of the church, such an occasion should be made a significant event by the minister and the church.

Walter Scott Athearn, one of America's foremost leaders in Christian education of a generation ago, once said, "If a boy or girl is not won for Christ by the time he or she is 21, the chances are three to one that he or she will not be won by anyone, any time, anywhere." Youth time is decision time. Very few, comparatively speaking, are ever won to Christ and for the church after they are 21 years of age. Speaking generally, about one fourth of our members make decisions before they are 13; about one fourth after they are 21; and one half between 12 and 21 years of age. This means that 75% of all members in our Protestant churches today became members before they were 21 years of age.

On one occasion when the late Dwight L. Moody was conducting a revival meeting in London, England, he returned to his hotel after an evening service. A man in the lobby said to him, "Mr. Moody, how many converts did you have tonight?"

Mr. Moody replied, "Two and a half."

"What do you mean," said his friend, "two men and a boy?"

"No," said Mr. Moody, "two boys and a man."

When you win a man to Christ, you win a unit. When you win a boy, you win a whole multiplication table. Youth time is decision time, whether in a personal, public acceptance of Christ or in anything else such as decisions concerning college, marriage, and the choice of one's lifework.

Nicodemus said to Jesus, "How can a man be born when he is old?" (John 3:4.) Jesus did not say in his reply that a man could not be born again when he was old. But church statistics and experience show conclusively that very few, comparatively speaking, are ever born again after they become old.

The term "salvation" is not fully understood by many. Its meaning is not clear. It means not only the saving of the lost, but the saving from loss. When parents, teachers, and pastors carefully instruct children with reference to the Bible, Christ, and the church, they are saving from loss. After instruction, then comes a personal commitment on the part of the child to become a conscious follower of Christ.

Perhaps pastors and teachers have not been making their appeal with sufficient urgency for the meeting of the spiritual needs of children today. They grow rapidly and before we realize it, they have become adults. The need for the enlistment and training of more teachers in Christian education is most urgent.

Someone says, "How urgent is the need?" The number of children under ten years of age has increased over 40% since 1940, while the general population has increased less than 15%.

Recently Gerald E. Knoff, executive secretary of the Division of Christian Education of the National Council of Churches, stated:

> As a Christian nation, we cannot afford to let a single child go without his spiritual heritage. All children need God and it is the task of parents and churches alike to give them every opportunity to weave spiritual and religious values into the fabric of their lives. The moral crisis faced by individuals and nations in our time can only be dealt with successfully upon a broad basis of spiritual training. That training should certainly begin in childhood with church and home leading the way.[3]

The median age of conversion 25 years ago was 16-17 years of age. Now it is 12-13. Conscious and public commitments to Christ on the part of boys and girls are made earlier in life now because of the better lesson materials with their evangelistic emphases in the junior years and the better evangelistic work on the part of teachers and pastors. Many ask the question, "How old should a child be before he or she unites with the church?" One might as well ask, "How tall should a child be or how much should he or she weigh before becoming a Christian?" It is not a question of weight, height, or age at all. It is a question of proper Christian teaching early in life. Some boys and girls because of proper teaching are more ready to become members of the church at 10 or 12 years of age than others are at the age of 16 or 17. It is interesting to note that William McKinley became a Christian when he was nine years of age, Frances E. Willard when she was 9, Robert Moffat when he was 8, and A. J. Gordon when he was 11. It is better to save by a lighthouse than by a lifesaving crew. Better to save by a

---

[3]Used by permission.

Sunday school than by a reform school. Church prevention is better than court cure. A church that cannot save its own children cannot hope to save the world. A man by the name of Dillinger was listed by the United States government as public enemy number one. At one time, when a lad in his early teens, he attended a small Indiana church school not far from Indianapolis. The writer talked to his church school teacher about this noted criminal. His comment, uttered in a sad voice, was, "If I had only done a better job in teaching that boy, he might have turned out to be a great man instead of a desperado."

Benjamin Kidd once said, "There are no heathen children. You can begin with any normal baby and teach it any language, reverence for any flag, or worship of any gods or God." If this is true, then we are always within one generation of realizing the kingdom of God on earth!

Watkinson of England once wrote that in the making of a Shasta daisy, five factors are involved—the sun paints it; the ocean gives it water to drink; gravity gives it shape; ether gives it vitality; and the earth gives it food. In bringing a child to a personal Christian commitment, these factors are involved— the home, the Bible, the church school teacher, the pastor, and the Holy Spirit.

Christian education and evangelism are inseparable. God has joined them together and what God has joined together, let not men put asunder. Christian education must have an evangelistic content to save it from becoming merely academic, formal, cold, and purposeless. On the other hand, evangelism must have an educational content in order to save it from mere emotionalism and superficiality. The question needs to be asked frequently, "Is our evangelism educational and is our education evangelistic?" The force of a shell fired from a gun is determined by the force back of it. Evangelism is the force back of

Christian education that gives it drive and direction.   Our Christian education needs to become saturated with the evangelistic spirit.

Do you have any underprivileged children in your community? Wait a minute before you answer with too much assurance. We are prone to think only of children who live with bare necessities of proper and healthful living as being underprivileged. They are not the only group of children who are underprivileged. The child without the advantage of the church; the child who does not have a Christian father or mother; the child whose parents send him to church and Sunday school instead of bringing him; the child who does not have encouragement from his or her parents to live a Christian life; the child who never hears his father or mother pray, sees or hears them read the Bible— these are the really underprivileged children in the community.

The denominations are doing more for the evangelism of childhood in America than ever before.   The same is true of the councils of churches, state and national, across the nation. Our seminaries are giving more and better training to our future ministers in Christian education.   Local congregations are sensing the tremendous responsibility that the children of the community put upon them for teaching and winning the children for Christ.   Many children of different races and colors in our country do not know the friend of all children—Jesus Christ—and his love for them.   Children are important to Christ and his kingdom.

CHAPTER 6

EVANGELISM OF YOUTH

In the Gospel of Mark, there is to be found the account of a conversation between Jesus and a rich young man. (Mark 10:17-22.) There is one phrase in this interview which is arresting. It is an observation made by the author of the Gospel of Mark, when he says, "And Jesus looking upon him loved him." How descriptive is this statement about Jesus. It not only indicates his attitude toward this young man, but it indicates his attitude toward all young people in any generation. He looks upon young people and loves them. As he challenged this young man to be his disciple, so today he wants and needs all young people everywhere to be his followers. It is my opinion that Jesus wanted this young man to be one of his apostles when he gave him the challenge to "go, sell what you have, and give to the poor, and you will have treasure in heaven; and come, follow me." As with many other young people since that time, the young man was not willing to accept the challenge. The record says, "At that saying his countenance fell, and he went away sorrowful; for he had great possessions." He simply was not willing to meet the demands of Jesus for discipleship, so he went away sorrowful, but he left a more sorrowful heart behind him.

This story, descriptive of a young potential disciple of Jesus, is a summons to all adults today to look at our twentieth-century youth through the eyes of Christ and love them as he loves them.

He did not love this young man with any superficial, sentimental love, but with a divine love that yearned for his companionship in his service.

From 13 to 24 years of age is considered youth time. This age includes the years from junior high through college. It is estimated that there are about 25,000,000 young people in America at the present time who are within this age bracket. This is more than one seventh of our population. This generation of youth, in many ways, is the finest America has ever produced. Without doubt the young people of today have stronger bodies, keener minds, and deeper spiritual insights than any generation this nation has ever known. Some feel that youth today has everything except a cause to which they can give themselves unitedly and enthusiastically. They have much to live with but no commanding cause to live for. Because of this lack of a sense of mission on the part of youth, someone has called them "the silent generation." They are not speaking up or speaking out about anything. We need to help them find a faith to live by, achieve a self fit to live with, discover a cause to live for, and co-operate with them in building a world fit to live in.

We talk and write much about the sins of our American young people. Of course, they are not angels and they do not want to be called angels, but they will respond to the highest and the best in life if given a real challenge. This generation, born of war and never weaned of pressures and tensions, is overwhelmingly decent and offers our nation more promises than problems. Our concern about youth has always been intense; today it seems to be obsessive.

Juvenile delinquency is causing widespread anxiety. But comparatively speaking, the great bulk of our young people are living and developing "in wisdom and stature and in favor with

God and man." They are growing toward responsible adulthood in a way that does credit to themselves, their parents, schools, country, and churches.

There *is* some juvenile delinquency. It must be recognized and dealt with wisely. During the six years from 1950 to 1956, the number of juvenile delinquents increased 29%. Fiftyone per cent of all persons convicted of crimes against property in 1954 were under 21 years of age. Of all persons arrested for auto theft in the cities that reported to the FBI, 62.2% were under 18 years of age.

One reason for delinquency is bad housing. Another is lack of playgrounds and supervision of recreation for youth. Still another is that in America there are over 3,000,000 boys and girls under 21 years of age, exclusive of those in the armed forces, who are not in school.

Perhaps the largest contributor to juvenile delinquency is the broken home and the lack of religious training in the home. If a boy or girl has a Christian home, where the father and mother set a good example by life and deed, the children are not likely to be delinquent. It is delinquent parents that make delinquent children.

The publishers of harmful comic books must take some of the blame for the present delinquency of many young people. There are 35,000,000 comic books read each month, two thirds of them by children and young people. There are approximately 300 different titles published each month. All comic books cannot be indicted. The Code of the Comics Magazine Association of America, adopted in September, 1954, and administered by a Code Authority, barred vulgarity, horror, terror, sex, sadism, and a number of other elements from the comics produced by its members who constitute 90% of the industry.

The perpetuation and continued success of the comics industry's self-regulation program is a matter of genuine importance to the public welfare. It is important that *only* those comic books which bear the Comics Code Authorities' Seal of Approval be bought, and distinguished from the others.

When we consider thoughtfully the kind of world youth is called upon to live in and which adults have built, we are bound to say that no generation of youth ever needed Christ more than this one. Anyone and everyone who is seeking to bring youth to Christ for a decision is in big business. Nothing is more important.

A research has revealed the following interesting comparison—when a gun-toting youth kills a man, it costs the state $125,000 to send him through the courts to the electric chair. If he gets a life term, it eventually costs double that amount. Thus one crime is equal in cost to a church building in which thousands each year may learn something about God and the sacredness of life.

"An ounce of prevention is worth a pound of cure" goes the old adage. The movements and organizations, to name only a few of them which are working with youth today to prevent delinquency and to build character, are:

Boy Scouts and Girl Scouts—Every church should have as many troops as possible. Every community needs to encourage and support scouting. These organizations are doing much to produce strong men and women. This world-wide organization helps both prevent and cure juvenile delinquency.

Baseball Leagues—For the teen-agers, baseball is a wholesome sport. Not many boys who are a part of this American sport get into trouble with the law when they have proper supervision. Many congregations over America have baseball teams and conduct interchurch games.

Our Public Schools—These are among the greatest institutions in our nation for character building. The games fostered by these schools such as track, baseball, basketball, and football teach fair play, co-operation, and clean living. With few exceptions our public school teachers all over America have a wholesome influence upon the students by both life and deed. Other wholesome programs for student participation carried on by our public schools in behalf of character building include drama, orchestras, and debates.

But greater than the influence on teen-age life by programs is the influence of a good teacher. William Stidger of Boston indicates the potential greatness of an intelligent public school teacher. He illustrates this by a true story about a sociology class of Johns Hopkins University which made a study of juvenile conditions in one of the slum sections of Baltimore. Two hundred cards, referring to some of the children in the schools, were marked "Headed for jail," by this sociology class. Twenty-five years later another class accepted the project of tracing those 200 cases. Only two of the 200 had ever been in jail. Aunt Hannah, an intelligent mother-hearted school-teacher of 40 years' faithful service, had taught the 200 in grade school. The writer says that man after man gave the testimony, "I *was* headed for jail until Aunt Hannah got hold of me and started me in the right direction." A single woman had counteracted the influence of the slums.

This is an adult world. Adults have made it and youth is having to live in the kind of world which adults have made and are making. Our young people of today do not make the liquor they are drinking; produce the undesirable motion pictures they are seeing; manufacture the cigarettes they are smoking; build the roadhouses they are frequenting; make the wars in which they are asked to fight; or write the salacious literature some of them are reading.   Where the young people of fifty years ago had one temptation in both rural and urban America, the young people of today have one hundred.   Hence, the young people of today need Christ more than any other generation. When their lives are committed to him, the policeman is put on the inside.   When this happens, a young person is controlled and motivated from within and not compelled from without.

There are many young people today on the college and university campuses of America.   It is reported that in the school year of 1954 there were over 2,500,000 enrolled.   In ten years, and this is worth thinking about, it is predicted that the number will be 4,000,000 to 6,000,000, and by 1970 there may be as many as 7,000,000 enrolled.

There is an upsurge of interest in religion among college students today.   Of 7,000 students at 12 colleges and universities, in a recent study 8 out of 10 said they felt the need of a religious faith.   Only 1 per cent described themselves as atheists.   Yale University offers 12 courses in biblical study.   In 1928 the University of Chicago employed one chaplain.   In 1956 it had 11 full-time and 13 part-time chaplains.   Princeton University in 1939 had 20 students enrolled in religious courses.   In 1956 700 were enrolled.   There is a growing feeling on the part of educators that knowledge without faith in God can be a dangerous thing.

There are a number of strong movements in America today which have as their dominant purpose the evangelism of youth. Some of these are:

The University Christian Mission—This is an organization within the Department of Evangelism of the National Council of Churches.   It was begun in 1938.   A budget of $23,000 annually is provided for this work on the college and university

campuses of America.   The Statement of Purpose for this
evangelistic movement among the students says:

> It aims to present in terms intelligible to university men
> and women, the relevance of the Christian faith, both to
> personal life and to the great social issues of this age. . . .
> It seeks to win students to an active Christian life and
> service in the church.   It aims to persuade them to a Chris-
> tian dedication in whatever vocation of social usefulness
> may be their calling.   It asks for devotion to Him who can
> release the flow of vital and unselfish energy by which man
> may attain freedom from the dominion of selfishness.   It
> points the way—the only way—by which, in common con-
> secration, men and women of the present generation may
> realize the peace for which they long.   For in His will is
> our peace.

The University Christian Mission goes to a college or university campus for one week.   Carefully selected speakers are
invited to become members of a team.   The number in the
teams varies from 5 to 25, depending on the size of the campus
student enrollment.   They have served and are now serving for
their expenses only.   These leaders speak in convocations, classrooms, and to student organizations of all kinds.   They hold
"bull sessions" in fraternities and sororities and conduct seminars on various vital themes.   During the past years there have
been some splendid results.   Faith has been deepened for many
students, church attendance has been increased, some have
united with the churches, a number have decided for full-time
Christian service, and on many campuses religion has been
made more respectable intellectually.   These missions are being
continued.   During the academic year 1955-56, 22 missions
were held.   On these 22 campuses the student enrollment was

60,000 and there were over 100 different guest speakers on the teams. Each of the past 18 years of these missions has averaged this many campuses in the schedule. Approximately 1,200 to 1,800 colleges and universities in the United States have a Christian mission annually. Many of these hold their own missions without outside help.

Christian Missions at Military Bases—Ever since the beginning of World War II, the Department of Evangelism of the National Council of Churches has been conducting Christian missions. Almost all those in training during World War II and since have been young men and women under 25 years of age. These missions were held for one week each. About 5 to 15 guest speakers were invited and used in each mission. The speakers received their entertainment and travel expenses only. These missions were held in order to assist the chaplains in their work. All plans for the missions were made with and through them. Many missions are now being conducted by the military units themselves. The Navy, Air Force, Army, and Marines have been very successful in their mission programs. Many missions are held annually by them. Through their chaplains, preparations are made, speakers invited, and the missions are carried on both at home and overseas.

Youth Missions—These are being conducted by the Department of Evangelism of the National Council of Churches for high school age young people of a given community. The churches of the community co-operate in this enterprise, which is usually three or four days in length. The young people in the high schools are reached through character-building messages in convocations and through high school organizations. The Christian message is presented interdenominationally to the young people of the community in discussion groups and in united church services in some church building.

Youth Work Camps—In these youth work camps, conducted in this country and in other nations, young people are given an opportunity to enrich their Christian faith, increase their understanding of the Bible, and give their Christian witness. These work camps are often interracial, interdenominational, and international in character.

Christian Youth Fellowships—Most communions have such youth organizations in almost all their respective congregations. Their weekly attendance runs into the millions. The communions provide printed guidance material for their young people. These Fellowships are an indispensable training ground for the youth of the churches by the churches. For the most part these Christian Youth Fellowships meet on Sunday evenings and are given adult leadership. These Fellowships not only contribute to the Christian growth of young people, but also they are a source for securing new members for the churches.

Christian Endeavor—Many churches have Christian Endeavor societies. This organization on all levels—national, state, county, and local—is evangelistic. Its motto for years has been, "For Christ and the Church." Countless numbers of young people have been brought into the membership of the churches of America since the movement was organized in Maine in 1881.

YMCA and YWCA—All through the years, these two organizations have been of significant help to millions of young men and women in almost every community in America. Through Bible study groups, lectures, night school classes, and recreational programs, the youth of the community have been saved not only from something but to something. The work of these two organizations has been and is constructive. They are "arms of the churches" and a blessing to the communities in which they serve.

Youth Conferences—One of the finest movements for young people is to be found in the many youth conferences which are held in America every year. These are conducted by the churches. Almost all of them are sponsored and administered by the denominations. Here again, through these conferences, there is an enrichment of Christian faith, a better understanding of the Bible, decisions for lifework, a greater knowledge of the church and what is happening in God's world. These conferences are an evangelistic agency and it is highly desirable that they become increasingly so.

The Church School—Perhaps almost all Christian leaders will agree that the church school is one of the most effective evangelistic agencies for the teaching and winning of youth to Christ and church membership. It is difficult to hold this age group in the church school. The attendance problem is largely solved by trained teachers who know the problems of youth and who really love them. Another solution to the attendance problem is found in the school's recreational and fellowship programs conducted for and by youth. The home is a part of the solution, for where fathers and mothers set the example by attending the church school regularly themselves, it is easier to keep young people regular in their attendance.

Youth Missions—Some congregations, encouraged and helped by their denominations, are conducting youth missions. The young people themselves, who are members of the churches, are trained and sent out two-by-two to call upon others of their own age. The First Methodist Church of Norwalk, Connecticut, recently sent out over 40 of its youth to call. Their goal was fourfold: (1) To find the unchurched youth; (2) to enroll youth in the Methodist Youth Fellowship; (3) to lead young people in a commitment to Christ; (4) to help them witness as Christians. The teams were advised to keep their conversa-

tions Christ-centered.   Methodists report that these youth missions are in their sixth year and that they are gaining mo-
mentum.   Of the 107 Methodist Conferences in the United
States about 100 have youth missions.   Other denominations
are using their young people in similar ways.

The evangelism of youth depends largely upon the adult
leadership of youth.   After all, nothing goes ahead of leadership.   If the leaders of youth groups in local churches are unconcerned about winning young people to Christ, or in training
them to win other youth, then few, if any, evangelistic results
will happen.   I was in a church recently attending a fellowship party of the young people.   In the group were four teen-
age boys, who had been in the group about a year.   When they
were first brought into the group they were "toughies," having
come out of a neighborhood gang.   But after one year with
the Christian young people of that church, the boys made their
confession of faith one Sunday evening and were baptized.

Paul once said to Timothy, "Let no man despise your youth."
(1 Timothy 4:12.)   From the beginning of the Christian
church on Pentecost, youth has played a significant role and
made remarkable contributions toward the progress of the kingdom of God.   Artists have often given the impression that the
12 apostles were old men.   Nothing could be farther from the
truth.   It is doubtful if any one of them was more than 25
years of age.   Students of evangelism are impressed with the
fact that the great evangelists were most effective in their earlier
years.   Jonathan Edwards led "the great awakening" in his
early thirties.   Charles Spurgeon, Charles G. Finney, and
Dwight L. Moody reached their crest of soul winning before
forty years of age.

Christianity has a particular appeal to youth in its call to
chivalry, courage, and adventure.   The inspiration of Christ's

personality was caught by many youthful leaders.   John Wesley
founded the Holy Club at Oxford at the age of 26.   Martin
Luther climbed the Scala Santa in Rome at 27.   Jeremy Taylor
was holding men spellbound in London at 18.   Francis E.
Clark founded Christian Endeavor at 29.   George Williams
founded the YMCA at 25, and David Livingstone was doing a
mighty work in the heart of Africa in the third decade of his
life.

"Trinity Echoes" gives the following ten commandments for
young people as a code of conduct—

> Stop and think before you drink.
> Don't let your parents down; they brought you up.
> Be humble enough to obey.   You will be giving orders
> yourself some day.
> At the first moment turn away from unclean thinking—
> at the first moment.
> Don't show off when driving.   If you want to race, go to
> Indianapolis.
> Choose a date who would make a good mate.
> Go to church faithfully.   The Creator gave us seven
> days in each week.   Give Him back one of them.
> Choose your companions carefully.   You are what they
> are.
> Avoid following the crowd.   Be an engine, not a caboose.
> Or even better, keep the original Ten Commandments.

Youth time is decision time.   It is in the earliest years of life
that most decisions are made for the later years of life.   Unless
young people are led to a decision for Christ and the church
by the time they are 24 years of age, it will be increasingly difficult if not almost impossible to lead them to such a decision
after that.

The choice of a lifework is made in youth.   There is much
that the churches can give to youth in the choice of vocations,
through the pastor and other leaders.   One emphasis needs

to be kept in mind—there is no such thing as sacred and secular work, if God is in it. All work is sacred if men and women bring God into the center of it and serve him through it. The work of the laborer, doctor, lawyer, merchant, manufacturer, farmer, teacher, nurse, author, editor, actor, or parents in the home, is just as sacred as being a minister or missionary, if God is brought into it and he is glorified through it.

Because of a disturbing shortage of ministers, missionaries, and directors of Christian education in our churches today, it is imperative for the churches to try to enlist more of our strongest young people for these three callings. The reason why more of our best are not thinking of these vocations is that, in many instances, no one has presented them seriously to our young people. These three vocations especially have much to do with the future of our evangelism for "how are men to call upon him in whom they have not believed? And how are they to believe in him of whom they have never heard? And how are they to hear without a preacher? And how can men preach unless they are sent?" (Romans 10:14-15.) There are many congregations which have not contributed one young person to the Christian ministry during this century. Yet, during this time they have had the services of ten or more ministers. This matter of ministerial recruitment must be taken seriously.

So many new congregations and Sunday schools, as has already been pointed out, are being organized today in new housing areas and elsewhere that a vigorous recruitment to man them must be carried on by all the churches. The number of young people now in our seminaries is not sufficient to replace those who are retiring and those who die.

CHAPTER 7

EVANGELISM OF ADULTS

There are two words that occur and recur in the first chapter of John's Gospel. One is the word "found" which occurs five times in the one chapter. It occurs once when Andrew "found" his brother Simon Peter and brought him to Jesus. Again, when Andrew says that he has "found" the Messiah; again, when Jesus "found" Philip, and also when Philip "found" Nathanael and said to him, "We have found him of whom Moses in the law and also the prophets wrote, Jesus of Nazareth, the son of Joseph."

The second word that occurs and recurs is the word "witness." It occurs five times in the same chapter. Evidently John the apostle could not forget the word of his Lord just before his ascension when he said, "You shall be my witnesses in Jerusalem and in all Judea and Samaria and to the end of the earth." (Acts 1:8.) This word "witness" stuck in his mind. A witness is someone who tells what he knows about a person or a thing. Jesus made sure that the twelve apostles were his qualified witnesses. They came to know him through their close association with him for about three years.

Today, as then, modern Christians are called upon to find others for Christ and to give them their unmistakable witness of him. There is an urgent need for faithful witnessing today. America is much like a courtroom. It has its seats for spectators and it also has its witness chair. The question comes to each Christian, "Am I in the seat of a spectator or am I in the witness chair telling others by life, word, and deed what I know about Christ?" There is a vast difference between being a witness of a trial and a witness at a trial. There is a serious trial going on in America today. Christ is once again in Pilate's judgment hall. Just before the crucifixion, our Lord stood alone before Pilate. No one was present, not even one disciple, to speak up for him or stand by him. Said the Psalmist, "Let the redeemed of the LORD say so." (Psalm 107:2.) There are many silent saints in our churches today, and there are many in the seats of spectators instead of in the witness chair.

In our evangelism at the present time, the churches face two major problems. One is that of securing a hearing for the message. The churches have the greatest message ever heard by man. It is the gospel, which is the "power of God for salvation to everyone who has faith." Most of the adults who are not members of any church today are not going to church; therefore, they are not hearing the message proclaimed from the pulpits of America every Sunday. The unchurched are not going to church today as they did sixty years ago. At that time there was scarcely any place to go on Sundays except to church. Things have changed. In those days there were no hard-surfaced roads in America, no automobiles, airplanes, radios, television sets, or motion picture theaters. It was not uncommon during the nineteenth century and in the early part of the twentieth for a church audience to be made up of many unchurched citizens of the community. They were present to hear the message. The preacher had an opportunity to teach, persuade, and win them to Christ. But today the situation is different. There is much in these modern times to attract and interest those who are members of no church, both through the week and on Sundays, so that very few of them attend church services except perhaps on very special occasions. The same situation is to be found in revival meetings and preaching missions. The attendance at these special meetings is made up almost entirely of church members. Even with the most popular and widely known preachers in the pulpits in any church, rural or urban, 95% or more of those present are already members of some church. There may be exceptions here and there, but not many. The hands raised and the cards signed in preaching missions or revival meetings often represent those who are already members of local churches and who desire to make a new commitment or a rededication of themselves to Christ and the church. Even though these things are true with reference to the unchurched, there is still a real place today for revival meetings and preaching missions. However, instead of holding these night-by-night meetings of two or more weeks with the unchurched in mind, these meetings should be planned for and held primarily for those who are already in the churches. Most congregations need a spiritual quickening and an awakening every now and then. More revival meetings of this kind need to be held. The sermons preached should be for those already members of the church. Such revivals or missions of two or more weeks could mean a rekindling of fires in many cold hearts.

The second major problem in evangelism is to get those who are unchurched to feel a sense of need. We say, and rightly so, "All men need Christ and the church." But not all men feel a sense of need of Christ and the church. It is often difficult to get people to want the *bread* of life, when they think they have cake to eat. It is difficult to get people to want to carry a *cross* when they are thinking of their personal comforts much of the time. There is a feeling of self-sufficiency and self-satisfaction on the part of many in America. In other words, they have no idea of personal lostness in the sense that Jesus used the term when he told the parables of the lost sheep, the lost coin, and the lost boy.

There is an answer to these two major problems. One is to be found quite largely in lay evangelism. It is possible for the churches to so select and train and use laymen and laywomen to do face-to-face evangelism that they become highly successful in reaching those who do not come to the churches to hear the Christian message from a pulpit. If people will not come to church to hear the message, then the church should take the message out to the people.

Another answer to the problem of reaching the unchurched is to be found in and through Christian education. An aggressive Christian education program that reaches out for new scholars, young and old, makes for larger evangelistic results. Homes where there is a concern for the teaching of the word of God to growing boys and girls is part of the answer. Church school teachers, who are well trained and deeply dedicated to their task of Christian education, are also part of the answer.

The other major problem—to get people to feel a sense of need—can be solved at least partly by presenting Christ to men and women one by one. This can be done by teachers in the church school; by preachers from the pulpit and by Christian friends. In the light of his presence they are able to see their need. Black never looks quite so black as when white is placed beside it. Isaiah did not get a vision of himself until first he experienced a vision of God. It was after he got a vision of God that he got a vision of himself. The psychologists tell us that what gets our attention gets us. Very few can withstand Christ and hold out against him if their attention is riveted on him for any length of time. The question that each must answer is Pilate's question, "What shall I do with Jesus?"

The lost word in most churches is the word "how." How do you reach the unchurched today? The method by which trained, dedicated laymen and laywomen are sent out two-by-two to share Christ with others is called "visitation evangelism." It is not a new method. It is as old as the New Testament. It is sometimes called, "operation doorbell." Jesus sent out the twelve apostles two-by-two. He sent out the seventy two-by-two. The wise church today is the one that will take this method of our Lord and use it seriously to reach the unchurched, interviewing them face to face for Christ in their homes, shops, stores, offices, and on the farms. This method is not the only method of evangelism, but it is the most effective one for reaching the unchurched multitudes in our day and time.

The writer gave his first public address on evangelism at a convention of his communion, Disciples of Christ, in St. Louis in 1920. Among other things, he said this, "We have been ringing church bells when we should be ringing doorbells; we have been doing by proxy what we should be doing by proximity, and we have been doing by purse what we should be doing in person." Jesus was no stranger to doorways or the market places of his time. He went out where people were. Our Lord preached often to multitudes in the synagogues, on mountain sides, and by the sea. But more often he gave his message to one person at a time. He had time for one individual at a time. Most of his healings were performed one at a time. There may be mass production in industry in America today, but there is no such thing as mass conversions. Men and women must decide for Christ one by one.

One very effective way to reach and win adults for Christ and the church is through the church school. Many adults through evangelistic teachers and through wide-awake adult Bible classes can be influenced to become members of the class. In it they become acquainted, form friendships, and become oriented to the church. The names of those in the adult classes who are not members of any church in the community should be placed on the evangelistic responsibility list for further and continual cultivation.

Some religious education leaders feel that the most important age group within the adult department is the group of young married people. Many feel that this group is more approachable and more easily won to Christ. These young fathers and mothers feel the weight of responsibility for the spiritual nurture and growth of their children. They want and need help. Every church, no matter how large or small, should have at least one class for young parents. Their children should be enrolled in the nursery, kindergarten, and primary departments. It is a wise church that makes adequate provision for the religious education of both children and parents.

There has never been a time in all the history of Christianity when there were as many laymen and laywomen who have been trained for personal evangelism by the Protestant churches as there are today. A conservative estimate would be 3,000,000 who have been trained and used in this, the greatest work in the world, during the past decade. If anyone wants to know why the Protestant churches in America today are growing twice as fast as the population, they can find the answer in the larger use of the laity in evangelism. These laymen and laywomen are trained for this evangelistic work by the pastors and sent out two-by-two under their direction. It is a fact that when laymen and laywomen are carefully selected and trained and used in this method of visitation evangelism, they get better and larger results ofttimes than their ministers. This has been proved over and over again. One of the reasons for this is that when a minister calls on a person to talk to him about his relationship to Christ and membership in the church, the one interviewed often has the feeling that the minister is talking to him because he is paid to do it. But when two laymen go, giving up an evening at home in order to make a call, the one called upon feels that this must be a very important matter if two people will do all this in his behalf without any remuneration. Also, laymen are successful in this work of person-to-person evangelism because they use a vocabulary that is not made up of theological words which the average unchurched person does not understand.

Perhaps a brief statement about the mechanics of visitation evangelism is appropriate at this point. It is a method that will work today in any church whether large or small, whether urban or rural. One of the secrets of success in lay evangelism is preparation. The degree of preparation determines the degree of success. In some instances, the church should take a year for adequate preparation in order to have a successful week of visitation evangelism, and in other instances, six months. The following are important items that need careful consideration and action:

Responsibility List—The unchurched of the community should be listed and then cultivated. Names and addresses are secured often by taking a door-to-door census. Wherever possible a community census should be taken interdenominationally. Also visitors at the church services should be asked to sign the register or fill out attendance cards. The church membership roll should be studied in order to discover members in families who do not belong to any church. Sunday school enrollment includes many who should be members of the church. The members of the church should be requested to turn in to the pastor the names of relatives, friends, and neighbors who should belong to the church. The process of continuous cultivation of the responsibility list should go on through friendly calling, by conversations over the telephone, and through the mails.

A word of exhortation to pastors and committees on evangelism in local congregations is appropriate just here with reference to the responsibility list. It is not easy to gather this list, secure information about it, and verify the addresses and telephone numbers. More often local churches fail in their work of evangelism because they do not have an adequate, cultivated responsibility list than for any other single reason, as far as the mechanics are concerned. It is hard work to gather such a list, to keep it up to date, and to cultivate it, yet it is absolutely necessary to do this if there are to be worthy evangelistic results.

The Workers—Select the workers for visitation with as much care as teachers or church officers are selected. Train them for this work. Prepare them through prayer. Give them pamphlets and booklets to read on the subject. Their first instruction period may well be held on a Sunday afternoon just preceding the week of visitation evangelism.

The number of trained workers needed in a local church may be arrived at in this way. If there are sixty names on the responsibility list, then four consecutive nights of calling would require five teams of two each. On an average, a team of two can make three calls in one evening. In order to keep these five teams busy for four consecutive nights, it would be necessary to have sixty names on the responsibility list. If there were 180 names on the responsibility list, then to call on every person even once would necessitate 15 teams of two each for four consecutive evenings of calling.

The Literature—Each Protestant communion has created a body of literature on visitation evangelism. This literature consists, among other things, of decision cards, prospect cards, pamphlets, booklets, and so forth. A three-cent stamp will bring to any pastor samples of needed literature from his denomination. In addition to literature, many communions have prepared filmstrips and turn-over charts for use by their churches.

The Suppers—Visitation evangelism will not succeed without the suppers, when the workers come together for fellowship about the tables on Monday, Tuesday, Wednesday, and Thursday nights. At this time, during or following the supper, the names of those on whom each team is to call are given out on cards. Further teaching on how to make a call is given at the table by the pastor or someone else, then a period of prayer and the benediction, following which the workers go out to make their calls. Those who serve the suppers during the four nights should be made to feel that their work is a very definite part of the evangelistic program and results.

Prayer—Lay evangelism will not succeed without a strong emphasis and a large place for prayer. In the Book of Acts, which is the greatest evangelistic book in the Bible, prayer is mentioned twenty-nine times. The early Christians went forward in their evangelism on their knees. They depended upon a power not their own. Prayer should be a definite part of all evangelistic plans of the church. This is especially necessary with reference to lay evangelism. Some congregations have a twenty-four-hour vigil of prayer on a Saturday night preceding a week of visitation evangelism, during which time there is intercessory prayer on behalf of those on the responsibility list and for those who are to interview them.

Many who are not able to go out to conduct the interviews for decisions are willing to accept a prayer list. Some churches form prayer groups which engage in daily prayer in homes or at the church during a week of visitation evangelism. Every evangelistic effort, no matter what program is to be followed or methods used, should be begun in prayer, continued in prayer, and ended in prayer. "More things are wrought by prayer" in evangelism than human minds can comprehend or fathom.

There are many other things that a pastor and his church must do in order to have commendable results in a week of visitation evangelism. The above five things are basic to success in reaching and winning the unreached for Christ and church membership.

It is strongly recommended that every church plan for and hold a week of visitation evangelism once each year. In addition to the five days (Sunday through Thursday) a church should plan one night a week for visitation evangelism for at least ten months out of the year. If this is not possible, then one night every two weeks or one night each month. Any rural or urban congregation that will take this method of visitation evangelism seriously will add converts to its membership. There are many churches in America that do not add even one new member to their numbers in a whole year. This is tragic. In such cases evangelism is neglected. The passionate spirit of evangelism is absent in such churches. What is the real purpose for a church's existence in a rural area or in an urban center, if it is not to evangelize?

The United Lutheran Church inaugurated a special evangelistic mission program in October, 1955, which will conclude in October, 1957. It is expected that by the end of the program every church of the denomination will have participated. The plans are unique in that every United Lutheran church in a given city or area invites a guest leader to help train the personal workers and to do the night-by-night preaching. Before the mission begins, the churches conduct an every-member visitation, requesting every member of every participating church to do three things—pray for the mission, attend every night, and bring some unchurched person.

The mission begins on a Sunday and concludes on the following Thursday evening. On four evenings from Monday through Thursday, those who are to go out to make personal soul-winning calls have a supper together. After supper instruction is given by the guest leader on how to make an evangelistic call. Each team of two is given two calls to make from seven to eight o'clock. Also, each team is expected to come to the church to attend the evening mission service to hear the guest missioner. Here is a combination of visitation evangelism and a preaching mission that is worthy of consideration by other communions which have never tried it. The leaders of the United Lutheran Church indicate that this plan is working very successfully, in that two things happen—first, the membership experiences a spiritual renewal and, second, new members are added to the churches.

A layman said recently, "In my opinion, a minister sins against his laymen and laywomen when he does not train and use them in the greatest work in the church—evangelism." He is right. To fail to use the laity in this soul-winning work is to rob them of the joy and the privilege of winning others to Christ. Increasingly the ministers of America are using this evangelistic method of visitation evangelism. A pastor friend of mine in Tyler, Texas, received 172 new members into his church on one Sunday following a week of visitation evangelism by a group of trained laymen and laywomen. After one year had passed, he checked on this fine group of new members to see if they were faithful to the church. He found that 134 were active, 23 had moved away, and only 15 were inactive. A number of the active members had important offices in the congregation in various organizations.

Samuel Morse felt that the War of 1812 might have been prevented if it had been possible to send a message across the Atlantic quickly. He spent most of the next twenty years trying to perfect an instrument to carry such a message, but still he could send a message but a few miles. At last he hit upon the solution—a relay. This meant a second telegraph key was operated by a signal from the first, a third by the second, and so on until the message had crossed the ocean circuit by circuit. Jesus found his personal ministry limited by the outreach of his voice and his lack of time. So he chose a relay system—his disciples. He might have said, "you shall be my relays." When the message of eternal life comes to us, we are under obligation to pass it on whether we are ministers or laymen. Through faith and prayer we can send out the fresh signal or we can let our spiritual batteries run down and the relay system die with us.

In 1945 in Greater Kansas City, forty congregations of one communion held a week of simultaneous visitation evangelism with the result that the forty congregations received 3,512 new members on one day. Here is one more indication that the laity of our churches are effective in winning others to Christ. In most instances all they need is leadership and training.

One night several years ago in Tacoma, Washington, two men called on a prominent judge. Being rather overawed because of the prominence of the judge in their community they started out in their interview by saying, "We are here tonight, Judge, to ask you to join our church." To which the judge replied, "Is that all you have to say?" Rather embarrassed, one of the men responded, "Well, frankly, we were told to approach this matter on a deeper level, but this is our first call and I suppose we took the line of least resistance." "I am very much interested in discussing this matter with both of you on the deeper level," said the judge. He continued, "Some things have caused me to think more deeply along spiritual lines than ever before." Thus encouraged, the two men began to relate their own experiences with Christ and found that they had much more to share than they would have dreamed possible. The judge made his decision and then surprised the men by saying, "Where are you going next?" They told him of their next call. He asked, "Would you mind if I went with you?" They readily assented and the three went to the next call together—or should it not be said that four went, since they were accompanied by the Unseen Companion who promised, "Lo, I am with you always."

In Peterborough, Ontario, Canada, a Baptist church conducted a week of visitation evangelism. Twenty trained workers participated. These secured 125 decisions. The pastor, following this large ingathering, presented to the church an effective assimilation program. Eleven months later he was able to report that of the 125 new members received, 119 were attending the services of the church faithfully. Eight of the number were teaching in the Sunday school; two had moved away and two were prevented from attending regularly because of illness. Of the 125 new members only two were inactive.

Visitation evangelism produces good results in military units. The chaplains at the Westover Air Base near Springfield, Massachusetts, called their special week of evangelism, "operation two-by-two." Seventy men were selected and trained as visitors to do the personal work. One third of this number were officers. A responsibility list of over 700 names was prepared of those at the Base who had never belonged to the church. At the end of the week, the chaplains reported that 233 had made decisions for Christ.

Several years ago, the Maple Street Congregational Church in Danvers, Massachusetts, in one week increased its membership

25 per cent by means of lay evangelism. The men and women of this church returned each evening with enthusiasm for their work. Some of their comments were, "I never thought they would join a church"; "I think we should do this every year"; "The people on our list were pleased to be asked to join the church." Before the prospective members were received into the membership of the church, they were required to attend seven classes of instruction given by the minister on successive Monday evenings.

In a recent evangelistic program in a New England city, the mayor welcomed the 200 people who were gathered for an instruction conference for the personal workers. He congratulated the group on their willingness to render this service and spoke of what it would mean to each one personally and to the people upon whom they called. After the meeting was over the mayor expressed his regrets to his pastor that official duties precluded his calling any night that week, but said, "It is only 4 o'clock now, give me some names and I will call this afternoon and tonight." The pastor gave him some names. He won eight of the nine persons whose names were given to him. In addition he called on two more who were his friends. He came to the manse at 10 o'clock that night with ten decisions for Christ and the church.

A Christian never quite realizes what the winning of one other person to Christ really means, both for time and eternity. It has far-reaching implications. Such work produces a chain reaction. One burning heart sets another heart on fire. As one reads the greatest evangelistic book in the Bible—The Acts of the Apostles—he is amazed at the rapidity with which the gospel spread and the way Christians multiplied.

I left my home on the farm at LeRoy, Kansas, in 1905 for Kansas University at Lawrence to study to be a doctor. I left home with $25 in my pocket. That $25 lasted me for six years at Kansas and Drake Universities. Of course, I had to do my part. I got a position in a Lawrence drugstore working afternoons, evenings, and on Saturdays in order to pay my way through the university. The owner of the drugstore was Harry L. Raymond, a good Baptist deacon. I had been in his employ about two weeks when he called me into his office and asked me this direct question, "May I inquire if you are a member of any church?" My reply, "Yes, I am and have been since I was 14 years of age." "I am glad to hear this," he said. "If there is anything I can do to help you in your Christian life, please let me know." I then asked this Christian man, "Do you ask every young man this question when he comes into your employ or have you singled me out for some reason or other?" "No," said he in reply, "I ask every boy this question who comes into my employ." I inquired further, "What have been your results?" His amazing reply was, "I have been in this store for twenty-two years. In that time I have employed many young men from the university and the city. Of all those who came to me who were not members of any church, I have been able to win every one of them to Christ, but two." What if every Christian employer would take that attitude toward every one of his employees? Why shouldn't every Christian employer take a religious interest in his employees? If every Christian employer in America would take a sincere religious interest in his employees, whether few or many, a religious awakening would come to this nation that would be without precedent.

Jesus said, "Go, make disciples," and many Christians would not need to go very far to begin. Perhaps across the street to a near neighbor, across the aisle in a department store, to an adjoining farm, to a friend in the same club or lodge, or to a friend on a college or university campus. Get somebody your size. If you are a banker, find a banker and win him to Christ. If you are a lawyer, find a lawyer; if a teacher, find a teacher; if a doctor, find a doctor; and if a farmer, find a farmer. There are so many within the social or friendship circle of every Christian who are members of no church. Up to now, there are a number to whom no word has been spoken personally. Someone asked Glen Cunningham, the famous miler, if he was a member of any church. His reply was, "No, I'm not." The questioner continued, "Would you mind telling me why you are not?" His answer was, "Simply because no one ever asked me." There are many hundreds like Glen Cunningham in America. They would become Christians and good ones, too, if someone took a religious interest in them and invited them to become followers of Christ and members of the church.

There are many unreached men and women in every community who would make just as good Christians as those in the church now—and in some instances better Christians. They need to be discovered and brought to Christ for salvation. He can do for them what he has done for us.

CHAPTER 8

EVANGELISM AND SOCIAL CHANGE

The Christian gospel has power, not only to change the lives of individuals, but to change the social order in which individuals must live. The social order is made up of units and these units are individual persons, created in the image of God. Personality is the pole around which the electrons of the social order revolve. The individual is still the fount and nexus of our social life.

We do not have a personal gospel and a social gospel. There is one gospel and one gospel only and that one gospel is the "dynamite of God." Paul says this about it, "For I am not ashamed of the gospel: it is the power of God for salvation to every one who has faith, to the Jew first and also to the Greek." (Romans 1:16.) It is the power of God not only for personal salvation, but also for family, community, economic, educational, racial, national, and international salvation. This indivisible message from God has its individual application and its social application. It has the power to redeem the individual and also the power to redeem the social order.

The personal and the social are not related as two hemispheres, but as cause to effect. Before there can be fruitage there must be rootage. A new person, with a new mind and a new heart, is first. The divine order seems to be new persons and then a better social order. It is impossible to get a brotherly world without brotherly men; to have a peaceful world without peaceful men or a better world without better men.

The General Assembly of the World Council of Churches, meeting in Evanston, Illinois, in 1954, stated,

> One [of our main concerns] is surely so to proclaim the gospel that it will transform the groupings and patterns of society in which men and women are involved, to the end that human institutions and structures may more nearly conform to the divine intention, and respect the limiting prerogative of God. We who think ourselves converted to the Christian gospel, and who have indeed entered into many of its blessings, should beware lest whole areas of our thought and outlook remain unregenerate, so that it is, after all, not the whole gospel to which we have been converted. No man is fully regenerate until he has brought every thought into captivity to the obedience of Christ.

In an editorial in *The Christian-Evangelist* Lin D. Cartwright said, "The A-bomb and the H-bomb are not dangerous. They are only things. What *is* horribly dangerous is unregenerate men. The control of these bombs is easy. If let alone, it is clear that they won't do anything. They will remain quietly in their boxes. What *is* needed is the control of man."

Only Christ-controlled men will ever be able to control the diabolical forces which are seeking to destroy our world. This makes the evangelization and the Christianization of men and nations an urgent matter.

If war is to be driven from the world, if illiteracy is to be banished, if poverty is to be eliminated, if disease is to be conquered, if race and class prejudices are to be dethroned, if the traffic in alcoholic beverages and narcotics is to be uprooted, and if all the other ills which scourge mankind are to be driven from the earth, the power for the accomplishing of all this must be found in the gospel of Jesus Christ and in the organization of committed Christians of all communities to unite themselves for the destruction of these evils. "The weapons of our warfare are not worldly but have divine power to destroy strongholds." (2 Corinthians 10:4.)

It is said of the first-century Christians, " 'These men who have turned the world upside down have come here also.' " (Acts 17:6.) These were the men "who had been with Jesus." They had caught his spirit and passion and they shared his concerns for the extension of his imperishable kingdom. They were new men, possessing new minds and hearts.

The General Assembly of the World Council of Churches said this significant word at Evanston, "The people of God are in this world as the Church, and they are never alone with their Lord in isolation from the world. It is the *World* which He came to save. Without the gospel the world is without sense, but without the world the gospel is without reality."

Now and then, some of the leaders in the area of social action within the churches feel that those who are concerned about evangelism do not place enough emphasis on the necessity for a better social order. There is some justification for this feeling. Often those concerned primarily for evangelism have nothing in their messages that would indicate that they are very much concerned about better housing, a living wage, improved working conditions, the eradication of race prejudice, the elimination of the traffic in narcotics and alcoholic beverages, and the destruction of the war system. On the other hand, the leaders in the area of evangelism often feel that those who are concerned about social action do not place enough emphasis on evangelism. Often there is no recognition in their writings or messages of the fact that redeemed persons are necessary for a redeemed society. It is possible for religious leaders to become so absorbed in social wrongs that they miss the deeper malady of personal sin. They lift the rod of oppression and leave the burden of personal guilt. They seek to correct social dislocations and overlook the tragic disorder of the soul. There is a social underworld because there is an underworld in man himself.

Some speak and act as though society were made up of something other than persons. The social order is made up of social units and the social unit is the individual. Our hesitation about evangelism, so far as it does not spring from a lack of clear conviction, is due to the false assumption that somehow we can get a better society without getting better men. We try to solve our social problems by some scheme and mass attack without getting at the root difficulties in the human heart.

In 1945 I traveled by plane from La Guardia Airport in New York to Casa Blanca on my way to Italy. My seat mate was a man from Ethiopia. He had been to San Francisco to attend a peace conference as a representative of his nation. I learned that he was a member of Haile Selassie's cabinet, in charge of education for the government. During our conversation I discovered that he was a member of the historic Coptic Church which traces its origin back to the church in Antioch in the Book of Acts of the New Testament. We talked much about World War II which was still going on at that time. Among other things I asked him this question, "Sir, would you tell me what you as a Christian statesman think is wrong with our world?" His reply was in one remarkable sentence, "Our intelligence, sir, has outrun our goodness." Just so. The culture of the mind in our day and time has outdistanced the culture of the heart. It is a tragic thing when men get science in their minds without Christ in their hearts. It is a question not only of how a man thinks but also how he feels, for "the heart is wiser than the intellect and moves with swifter hands and surer feet, toward wise conclusions."

General Omar Bradley has said, "We have too many men of science, too few men of God. We have grasped the mystery of the atom and rejected the Sermon on the Mount. Man has stumbled blindly through a spiritual darkness while toying with the precarious secrets of life and death. The world has achieved brilliance without wisdom, and power without conscience. Ours is a world of nuclear giants and ethical infants."

While the church as a church should not participate in politics, yet the church must always be the conscience of the state and society. The church cannot and dare not align itself with any system of government or political society. The church is to be concerned always, not only with reference to better persons, but also with a more Christian social order. Anything that has to do with human personality must be a concern of the churches. Christians are not only members of the church but they are citizens of their nation and of the world and as such should take an active interest in politics and in all organizations and movements that have for their purpose a more Christian social order.

The church has a gospel and this gospel must express itself through social action. Society, wherever evil exists in it, can be changed if and when Christians really want to change it. Organized Christians, when given bold leadership and when fired by a holy determination, can put evil to rout in any community in America. Jesus said, "Upon this rock I will build my church; and the gates of hell shall not prevail against it." (Matthew 16:18—KJV.) Jesus is stating quite plainly in this verse that when his church marches out unitedly and storms the gates of iniquity, these gates cannot stand. This has been demonstrated again and again. Truth is stronger than error, light is stronger than darkness, and love is stronger than hate.

Within our social order in the United States there are many organizations, movements, and institutions that strengthen the social order. They are life giving. They serve the people un-selfishly in the spirit of Christ. The oldest and best-serving in-stitution within our nation is the church. What would our na-tion be without it? This divine-human institution is a creative source of goodness and spiritual power. Its presence and service among us, blesses us from the cradle to the grave.

There are other organizations and institutions among us which men have created. Some of these are our schools, hos-pitals, the Red Cross, homes for children and old people, lodges, clubs, labor organizations, and so forth. Our system of govern-ment, on the national, state, and community level, while not perfect, is among the best in the world.

On the other hand, there are a number of evils at work within our social order in America. Sometimes these evils organize themselves into movements and institutions. The hand of the church must ever be against these evils until they are destroyed root and branch. There are many of these evils among us that should have consideration in this chapter, but limited space means that only a few can be mentioned and treated briefly.

One of the evils that plague us is race prejudice. Large holes are being made in the walls of segregation. Twenty-five years from now the picture will look more Christian. Increasingly, this nation is putting into actual practice the statement of the Apostle Paul on Mars Hill when he declared, "And he made from one every nation of men to live on all the face of the earth." (Acts 17:26.) The gospel has many things to say about the way man should treat his fellow man, regardless of his color, language, or nationality.

On May 17, 1954, the Supreme Court of the United States, by unanimous vote, held that segregation in the public schools violates the Constitution. Its ruling on its decision states: "Segregation of children in the public schools solely on the basis of race. . . deprives the children of the minority group of equal educational opportunity," and so is unconstitutional. Americans need to practice their democracy. A citizen is a citizen, whether black, white, red, yellow, or brown. No one living under the Stars and Stripes should be considered a second-class citizen, or made to feel that he is such. The gospel of Christ has to do with both our relationship to God through Christ and our relationship with our fellow man. The first relationship is perpendicular and the other horizontal. Every person everywhere is a person for whom Christ died. This truth should make all the difference in the world, in the attitude we have toward those of other colors and races. There are no inferior races. There are only backward races. Any race of men will go as far as any other race, if given the same length of time and the same opportunity. Those of the white race should not forget that they are where they are in their Christian interpretation of life because a man by the name of Paul went west instead of east. Had he gone east with the Christian gospel, India, China, and other eastern nations would have become Christian under the influence and power of the Christian message.

Another evil of today is the traffic in alcoholic beverages. This business has made great progress in America since the repeal of the eighteenth amendment. Americans are spending about $10,000,000,000 annually for alcoholic beverages. This is an average of $60 per capita for every man, woman, and child in the nation. There are about 4,500,000 alcoholics and this number is increasing at the rate of 50,000 annually. The Yale School of Alcoholic Studies estimates that there are 7,000,000 Americans who are out-of-control drinkers at present. They affect the lives of about 30,000,000 close relatives.

The liquor industry is spending about $250,000,000 per year in advertising, seeking to teach people to drink. This is done on the radio, television, in newspapers and magazines, and on billboards. Alcohol is a poison and acts upon the brain as an anesthetic. Dr. Frederick Lemere, a Seattle psychiatrist and neurologist, says, "Alcohol is a habit-forming drug and should be grouped with narcotics and barbiturates for it can produce physical as well as psychological habituation."

The total percentage of drinking Americans is rising steadily. Of all adult Americans it is estimated that 64 per cent drink. Alcohol is a social menace. The International Convention of the Christian Churches (Disciples of Christ) recently passed a resolution stating, "It is our conviction that to legalize the manufacture of a product which has such disastrous consequences for so many persons is in itself an antisocial and evil policy."

The Methodist Board of Temperance states, "More than 60% of all arrests made by the police in the first six months of 1956 were due to crimes directly related to alcoholic beverages. During the four holidays of Christmas in 1956, over 700 persons were killed by automobiles on American highways. Alcohol was responsible for many of these tragic deaths."

Upton Sinclair, Pulitzer prize winner, has written a book entitled *The Cup of Fury,* on the devastating effects of alcoholic beverages on forty American celebrities. He names them and writes about them. He says this of the liquor business:

Alcoholism *is* a disease, of course. But it scarcely seems to me that this excuses or clears the distillers of responsibility. Cancer does not advertise itself as a symbol of "thoughtful hospitality"; heart disease does not spend a quarter of a billion dollars annually to announce that it is an "aid to gracious living." Neither polio nor tuberculosis describe themselves in handsome posters and colorful magazine-spreads as a means to healthful relaxation and enjoyment.[2]

[2] Used by permission of Upton Sinclair and Channel Press.

This book is a documented, slashing exposé of the liquor industry and its attempts to make drinking a "social grace." It is a poignant record of despair and degradation caused by drink. A startling sentence in the book is this—"Three out of four of today's college students are drinkers." It is hard to believe that this is true.

The time has come when some group of Christians or some communion or, better still, the National Council of Churches of Christ in the United States of America with its 30 communions and 35,000,000 members, should rise up against this monstrous evil in our American life and drive it from our nation. Unless and until this evil is driven from our land, health will be impaired, minds will be wrecked, homes will be destroyed, crime will increase, alcoholics will multiply, deaths on the highways will rise, and the future of our youth will be threatened. The manufacture, sale, and use of alcoholic beverages is a national menace and it should be recognized as such by all Christians.

Atoms and alcoholic beverages do not mix. This fact is causing real concern, especially since General Nathan Twining, our Air Force Chief of Staff, in Washington, has reported on his visit to Russia in 1956. He expressed apprehension that drunken Russian Communist leaders could "plunge the world into war while drunk at midnight and might never remember anything about it the next morning." While men are drunk, they are not normal and their decisions can be dangerous. In an atomic era there is no place for a leader who is a slave to alcohol. This is true whether it concerns military leaders in Russia, London, or Washington. It is not to the credit of America that the largest per capita consumption of alcoholic beverages in our nation, so it is reported, is in the national capital—Washington, D. C.

The war system has scourged mankind for centuries—Jesus our Lord said, "Blessed are the peacemakers." Not, blessed are the peace talkers or the peace writers, but rather the *peacemakers*. If and when men and nations put as much time, money, and effort into the cause of peace as they do into war, then world peace will be a brighter possibility.

Recently the *United States News and World Report* computed that 1,130,393 men were killed in all American wars since 1776, and 1,276,520 others were wounded. No one can measure the human anguish, misery, and grief associated with 2,500,000 casualties. The cost in money and property for wars fought by the United States runs into billions of dollars.

What could not be accomplished with the billions of dollars now being spent and allotted to military budgets among the nations, if these dollars were to be spent for slum clearance, better housing, medical research, hospitals, safer highways, church extension, education, and world missions. Someday a generation will inhabit this planet with enough Christian faith, common sense, statesmanship, and a realistic awareness of the futility of war to do away with this ghastly business. Christians today in all lands need to pray and work for world peace.

Until and unless there is a universal disarmament agreement adhered to strictly among the nations, and unless and until there is a will to world peace on the part of the larger nations, our nation must be prepared to defend herself militarily against any aggressor. After saying this, one must go on to say that America's greatest defense is not in military might, but in her moral and spiritual strength.

Our best hope today for world peace, next to the churches, is in the United Nations. It is not a perfect instrument, but it is the best mankind has ever been able to provide. It was on October 24, 1945, that the United Nations Charter came into being. During its first eleven years it has helped to end civil wars in Greece and Korea, and has brought a truce in the war between India and Pakistan over Kashmir. It has arranged cease-fire agreements between Great Britain, France, Israel, and Egypt. It helped Iran, Lebanon, Syria, and Burma speed the departure of foreign troops from their soil. The United Nations is an invaluable forum for increased international understanding. At the present time (1957), 80 nations belong to the United Nations. Not only has the United Nations prevented wars but it has promoted peace, understanding, health, better human relations, and a hundred other good things.

Because of their interest in world peace, the churches should observe United Nations Week annually. Almost all the churches of America have been interested in this world organization from its beginning. The Protestant churches through the Department of International Justice and Goodwill of the former Federal Council had much to do with helping to write the charter. This Department, since 1908, has worked incessantly for world peace. Through the Commission of the Churches on International Affairs, which is a joint Commission of the International Missionary Council and the World Council of Churches, much is being done by the churches of 165 communions located in 50 countries of the world toward world peace. This Commission is in close touch with the United Nations and the capitals of many nations of the world.

In Caesar's day it cost 75 cents to kill a man in battle. In Napoleon's day the cost had increased to $3,000. It is estimated that it averaged $21,000 to kill an enemy soldier in World War I. In World War II America paid the equivalent of $50,000 per capita to kill her enemies. It can be seen clearly that the cost of war has mounted and in this direction is the financial bankruptcy of nations. Of every income tax dollar paid our Federal Government last year, three fourths went to pay for wars past, present, and future.

There is an International Peace Garden on the boundary line between the United States and Canada. The location is almost the exact center between the Atlantic and Pacific Oceans and only thirty miles north of the exact center of the North American continent which is at Rugby, North Dakota. The Province of Manitoba, Canada, gave about 1,400 acres, and the state of North Dakota gave about 1,000 acres for this Garden. The Garden is beautifully landscaped. Some nations sent their flowers, and others sent their shrubs and trees. On a bronze plaque situated in the center of the Garden are these words, "We two nations dedicate this Garden and pledge ourselves that as long as man shall live, we will not take up arms against one another." On the 3,000-mile boundary line between Canada and the United States there is not a soldier, gun or fort today, *but* a Peace Garden. May the day soon come when there will be a Peace Garden on every national boundary line of the world. May the followers of the Prince of Peace seek to help him make this a possibility.

Another well-known symbol of peace is found in South America. On the boundary line between Argentina and Chile stands the famous statue—the Christ of the Andes. This 26-foot statue was erected in 1904. Four years before its erection, these two countries were on the verge of war because of a disputed mountain boundary. The plaque at the base of the statue reads, "Sooner shall these mountains crumble into dust than Chile and Argentina break the peace to which they have sworn at the feet of Christ the Redeemer." May God hasten the day when the prophecy of Isaiah shall become a reality—

. . . they shall beat their swords into plowshares,
    and their spears into pruning hooks;

nation shall not lift up sword against nation,

> neither shall they learn war any more.   (Isaiah 2:4.)

World peace is possible.   War is not inevitable.

There is a serious crime situation in America.   Every sober-minded Christian citizen, especially, must feel a deep concern over the increase of lawlessness and crime.   Crime covers our nation like a blanket.   In 1956, J. Edgar Hoover, head of the FBI, stated,

> "Our record of law violation has become a national disgrace.   Today, one out of every 16 persons in the United States has been arrested and fingerprinted, while one out of every 31 persons has been convicted of one or more violations of the law.   One family out of 19 was affected in some manner by crime last year.   The enormity of the crime problem is reflected by the fact that for every dollar spent on education, one dollar and eighty-two cents is diverted to the cost of crime.   For every dollar given to the churches, crime costs us ten dollars."

Mr. Hoover goes on to paint this dark picture when he says,

> "Last year there occurred one major crime every four minutes, 15 every hour, 360 every day and 131,400 for the year.   In those brief twelve months, we had one burglary every 1.2 seconds; one robbery every 8.3 minutes; one larceny every 25.6 seconds; one rape every 29.4 minutes; one aggravated assault every 5.7 minutes; one automobile theft every 2.3 minutes and one felonious homicide every 41 minutes.   Every 24 hours, during last year, there occurred 35 murders, 49 cases of rape and 254 cases of aggravated assault."

Where is the remedy for our present crime situation? Of course, no one has all the answers to this gigantic problem, but perhaps some of the solutions lie in the following direction— more and better Christian homes; more children and young people receiving religious instruction; an increased church attendance; eradication of the liquor traffic; better law enforcement; a deeper respect for law and order; and a larger program for the evangelization of America.

To accomplish this new persons are needed, with new minds and hearts. It will be possible to have a better and a more Christian social order when we have more and better Christians in America and when these Christians organize themselves with determination to drive out these evils from our midst. Evangelism has a major part to perform in the changing of the social order since it is through the Christian gospel that men are made new persons and also motivated to do the will of God on earth. Every weed in the hands of a Burbank is a possible flower and every sinner in the hands of Jesus Christ is a possible saint.

CHAPTER 9

MASS MEDIA IN EVANGELISM

The churches have the greatest message the world has ever heard. It is the changeless gospel of Christ. It is the Good News from God to man for all men. It is not to be stored up but to be scattered abroad; not to be defended but to be declared; not to be protected but to be preached; not to be conserved but to be communicated.

One of the primary functions of the Protestant churches is the communication of this Good News from God. There are many methods by which this is done and there are many modern instruments available to the churches for this purpose which science has put into their hands. In this chapter these instruments will be given consideration, with reference to the communication of the Good News.

There are those who feel that if the power to evangelize is lacking, it is not primarily because the churches of different communions are in conflict with each other over matters of doctrine. Divisions over doctrine are often to be found more sharply *within* each communion than *between* the communions. The difficulty is not that a representative group of denominational leaders cannot produce an agreed statement of doctrine covering many important matters, but that when they have done it, nobody inside the churches seems to be the slightest bit impressed. The problem is one of communication.

The churches have an unprecedented access today to facilities of modern mass media such as the press, radio, television, and films for the preaching and teaching of the Christian gospel. It is amazing to think that one American preacher speaking over a network broadcast on a Sunday morning, preaches to many more people in 30 minutes than Paul did in a whole lifetime. John Wesley said, "The world is my parish." This statement is more true now than in his day, for we can reach the entire world parish today with the Christian message by means of modern mass media. It will not be long until there will be frequent international radio and television networks for the purpose of bringing the gospel to all who have radio and television receiving sets. Language barriers will be overcome through translations.

By means of radio and television a speaker can go through shut doors with the Christian message. Jesus needed to go through shut doors following his resurrection in order to speak with his timid disciples, and he did. Fear put the disciples behind those closed doors. We read of this incident in the Fourth Gospel, "Eight days later, his disciples were again in the house, and Thomas was with them. The doors were shut, but Jesus came and stood among them, and said, 'Peace be with you.'" (John 20:26.) For the first time in history messengers of the gospel may go through closed doors by the miracle of radio and television. By means of these modern media of communication a speaker or singer can go through closed doors to friends and even to enemies.

One of the most important things to consider always with reference to the use of mass media when you do go through closed doors, is to have something to say that is worth saying and in a language that is understood. We are told that the 500 most commonly used English words have 14,071 dictionary meanings. Words often have different meanings to different people. The Apostle Paul says, "If I do not know the meaning of the language, I shall be a foreigner to the speaker and the speaker a foreigner to me." (1 Corinthians 14:11.) By means of radio and television today we are slowly learning to understand each other's language.

Radio, as we now know it, was born in a garage in Pittsburgh in 1920. It soon became a force in the life of the world. Sometimes it has been used as a force for good and at other times for evil. Radio helped to bring Hitler and Mussolini to power. It can be used by a Communist for the propagation of his materialistic atheism or by a Christian for the propagation of the message of eternal life for the present and the future.

The use of the radio is not declining. There are more radio listeners today than there were before television. The average family spends two hours and nineteen minutes each day listening to a radio. In nontelevision homes, the radio is listened to over four hours daily and about one hour and forty-four minutes each day in homes where there is also television. In 1956, 14,000,000 radios were made—almost twice as many as television sets. Another surprising fact is that the number of radios in automobiles exceeds the total circulation of all morning daily newspapers in the United States. In 1956 there were over 3,000 radio stations throughout America, which is nearly three times the number in operation ten years previously. It is reported that the local radio income in 1955 was $320,000,000, more than twice the amount of total income in 1945.

It is estimated that at present there are about 98,000,000 home radios; 31,000,000 car radios; 1,000,000 sets in institutions, dormitories, military barracks and 5,000,000 in other places, or a total of 135,000,000 radio receivers in this country. These figures are eloquent when the churches seriously consider the possibilities presented by these many radios for the communication of the gospel.

I can remember the time during my university days when John R. Mott, Robert E. Speer, Sherwood Eddy, and Raymond Robbins came to the campus. Their theme was "The evangelization of the world in this generation." If these intrepid leaders felt in those days that the world could be evangelized in one generation with the limited resources at their command, what should be our expectations now with the vastly increased resources at our command? By means of our modern mass media we can get a message to the person living farthest from us in less than a second. Sometime in the not too distant future a generation of Christians will take Christ's command to "go . . . make disciples" so seriously, that it will attempt the evangelization and Christianization of the whole world in one generation.

Television is growing rapidly. As of 1955, there were over 400 television stations in the United States and in 1956 there was a total of 40,000,000 television sets in use. In 1955 there were 7,750,000 television sets made. About 75% of the total homes in our nation have television sets. The increase has been at the rate of 5,000,000 each year. The medium of television is young, having begun in about 1948. It has fantastic possibilities for use by the churches in the communication of the Christian gospel.

It was on the evening of November 27, 1956, that a nationwide NBC television program, "March of Medicine," was shown. Dr. John E. Ross, medical missionary of Disciples of Christ serving in Belgian Congo, and his hospital work were featured. It was an hour-long TV sound film. It told the story of modern medicine as it is carried on in a jungle village 80 miles east of the mouth of the Congo River and 100 miles up the Momboyo tributary. He is the only resident physician and surgeon for the village of 1,000 and for an area 250 miles up and for 50 miles down the river. He supervises the 200-bed mission hospital at Lotumbe and a leprosarium for 200 additional patients. This one-hour TV showing brought a vivid picture of medical missions to millions, and Dr. Ross's name became a household word all over America overnight.

Television is a big attraction for children. They spend an average of 26 hours per week watching their sets as compared with an average of 24 hours per week in the classrooms of the public schools and one hour each week in a Sunday school. In homes where there is television the average number of hours per day given to television is reported to be about five hours and 24 minutes.

By means of the radio and television the churches can reach the shut-outs as well as the shut-ins. The shut-outs are those who have had no contact with the churches and who know little or nothing of the program and life of the church. The shut-ins are those with church-related backgrounds who are now confined to their homes because of illness or age.

Radio and television are God-given miracles of communication for such a time as this. These modern instruments can be used to communicate the Christian gospel in order to:

reach the people for whom life has become a meaningless blur
find the people who have no faith to live by
discover the fearful and the insecure
seek out the lonely, the forsaken, and the friendless
reach those who are on the move
enlighten the misinformed with information about the church
stimulate thoughtless Christians to rediscover their faith
win others to Christ and church membership

The churches have come a long way since 1923. In that year the Federal Council of Churches had programs on three radio stations. Today, 1956, through the Broadcasting and Film Commission, the National Council of Churches, representing 30 communions with memberships totaling 35,000,000, has weekly programs on 852 radio stations representing the facilities of four national networks. Also these churches, through this commission, have television programs on 80% of the 430 or more television stations. In addition to all this, there are many radio and television stations in local communities carrying special religious programs.

One of the pitfalls in mass communication of the Christian gospel through radio and television and films especially is how to avoid mediocrity. Here the *good* can become the enemy of the best. There is no place for religious soap operas today through mass media of any kind. The Christian message calls for the best in talent and a great investment in money. There is a struggle going on in the world today for the minds and hearts of men, hence we must evangelize by *all* means. "By *all* means" certainly includes every instrument that science has made available to the churches, such as radio, television, films, and the printed word.

It is my conviction that radio, television, and the press can be used to prepare a community for evangelism. Especially is this true when preparations are being made for a special united evangelistic program. These modern media can be used for several months to prepare the minds and hearts of the community prior to a united program such as visitation evangelism, a preaching mission, or a teaching mission.

Good evangelism depends much upon Christian teaching. It would seem that modern mass media can be more and more used for teaching the Bible to childhood and youth especially. Here is a whole area that the churches have only begun to explore. More and better religious films, filmstrips and slides are needed as aids to be used by the churches in their teaching ministry.

Special training needs to be given in the Bible colleges and seminaries to our young men and women, not only on how best to use these modern instruments, but to know also what materials are available and where and how to order them. Our young ministers need to be taught, not only to preach, but how to speak effectively on the radio and television. The preacher of the future will be one who not only knows how to preach well from his pulpit but who will also know how to be an effective speaker on the radio and television.

There are certain things that must be remembered about this incredible electronic tool. It is necessary to keep in mind at all times when using it, that it *is* mass communication. One cannot single out any one group. One cannot say this program is for Presbyterians, Baptists, Lutherans, Methodists, or Disciples of Christ. Nor can one say any religious program is presented for Indians, Mexicans, Negroes, or Japanese. Television and radio religious programs must be available and adaptable to all groups and serve all groups within our nation. The churches should look upon these media of communication as inseparable parts of the churches' outreach.

It is surprising to find that many people, who do not go to church and who are not members of any church, listen to religious broadcasts. Some listen regularly. They have their favorite radio and television preacher and can tell why they like to listen to him. Comparatively speaking, there are not many conversions as a result of radio and television preaching, but there are a few. Not many radio or television listeners in America have united with the churches because of the preaching they have heard over these facilities. One of the greatest contributions radio and television preaching has made and is making is to keep faith in God alive in the hearts of millions. Perhaps one reason why more persons in a listening audience are not "converted and join a church" is that the churches have not worked out a follow-up plan. The Missouri Synod Lutheran Church has worked out a rather remarkable follow-up program. The speaker on the radio or television requests that letters be sent in, following the broadcast. The names of those writing in are sent to the Lutheran pastor who is ministering in a church in the community in which the writers of the letters live. He makes a call by phone or in the home on every one. In this way many unchurched people are reached for Christ and church membership.

The weakness today in Protestant broadcasting is not with the preachers who are selected to give the Christian messages, but rather it is to be found in our failure to provide sufficient funds and a follow-up program so that every one who writes in to any station, whether on the local or national level, will receive personal and prompt attention.

Concerning films, the producers of motion pictures are making more and better religious films than ever before. Some of these films have made a tremendous evangelistic impact upon the thousands who have seen them in theatres and in churches. The film, *A Man Called Peter,* was very popular. Among the productions of Twentieth Century-Fox for 1955, it stood at the head of the list of box-office champions. It cost $1,500,000 to produce it. It is one of the few religious films that deals importantly with religion. In this picture Richard Todd played the part of Peter Marshall. Mr. Todd's characterization was most memorable when he was acting as a minister of God's word in his pulpit. In the film Peter preached four remarkable sermons, ranging from the majesty of death to the reasons for belief in the existence of God.

It is reported on good authority that the Hollywood producers have never made a *good* religious film that has lost money.

Pictures such as *The Robe, Going My Way, The Ten Command-ments, Stars in My Crown, King of Kings, A Man Called Peter, Battle Hymn,* and others have all made money.

Other religious films that have been seen by millions are *Martin Luther, John Wesley,* and *Our Bible—How It Came to Us.* The first was produced under the direction of the Lutheran Church, the second under the sponsorship of the Methodist Church and the third by the American Bible Society. These films are educational, entertaining, and evangelistic.

Other widely viewed religious films have been produced by Billy Graham. Three of these are *Oil Town, Mr. Texas,* and *Souls in Conflict.* Following the showing of these films, the lights are turned on, then someone steps forward and announces an invitation hymn. Those present who desire to accept Christ or rededicate their lives to him are invited to come to the front of the hall. Many respond.

The churches of America are providing themselves with equipment for audio-visuals. Expenditures for audio-visuals were 20 to 40 times more in 1955 than in 1945. It is estimated that 60% of the local churches in the United States own or have access to 16 mm. motion picture projectors. A 1955 list, assembled by Eastman Kodak Research Department, indicates there are at least 1,300 religious films available to the churches, the majority of which were especially made for church use. Of those dated, over 85% were produced in the 1945-55 period.

Most of the denominations work with and through the Broad-casting and Film Commission of the National Council of Churches. The 1956 budget of this Commission was $1,751,400. In terms both of extent of expenditure and of cooperative activities this Commission ranks as the largest educational and promotional undertaking in the area of organized religion. It also stands today among the most important in the entire audio-visual field.

Our nation has been geared almost exclusively to the printing press since its invention back in the Middle Ages. Most of our culture has come through the printing press; most of our cultural heritage has been preserved through the printing press. However, we have come to a time in the use of modern mass media, which adds sight to sound and pictures to the printed word, and when we are developing mass communications media whose full dimensions or full implications we do not yet know.

The Protestant churches of America have been and are now using the printing press for strengthening the churches and extending the kingdom of God. Some of the publications are interdenominational and have a wide circulation. All the denominations have weekly journals and monthly magazines. In this way religious articles, up-to-date news and pictures are made available to the churches. A vast amount of religious education material is printed for the home, the Sunday church school, and weekday religious instruction classes. In many other ways the Christian message is interpreted for the strengthening of the churches both numerically and spiritually.

Some churches give a year's subscription to their denominational weekly or monthly publication to each new member as a part of the evangelistic conservation program.

America has 1,800 daily newspapers, many weekly papers, and numerous magazines. There has never been a time in the history of our nation when this medium of communication has given more space and more sympathetic attention to religion than now. All this helps to create a favorable climate in which the churches may do their evangelistic work.

Norman Vincent Peale has a syndicated column, entitled "Confident Living," which appears regularly in 150 newspapers. His monthly magazine *Guideposts* has a circulation of 625,000. Almost a million copies of his book, *The Power of Positive*

Thinking, have been sold.   Billy Graham writes a column entitled "My Answer" which appears in 200 daily newspapers.

Reader's Digest has one or more religious articles in every monthly issue. *The Saturday Evening Post, The Ladies' Home Journal, Look, Life, Coronet, Time,* and many other magazines carry frequent articles on the Christian religion.   In other words, religion is news.   Many editors of newspapers and magazines are Christians, hence understand how necessary Christian faith and the churches are to the well-being of America.   The same thing is true of book publishers.   They are printing more religious books than at any other time in the history of America. One reason for this is the *demand* for religious books.   Thus, the modern printing press and the publishers are helping to evangelize America.

In 1936 the writer directed a four-day preaching mission in St. Louis, Missouri.   The *St. Louis Globe-Democrat* gave unusual space to the mission.   They promised the local publicity committee, rather jokingly at first, that if the St. Louis Cardinals won the baseball pennant that year, they would give as much space to the mission as they expected to give to the World Series. The Cardinals did win and the *St. Louis Globe-Democrat* kept its promise.   On each of three consecutive days, they gave a four-page supplement to publish news of the mission, and on the fourth and last day of the mission a two-page supplement.

Life magazine, a few years ago, published some pictures of Dr. Albert Schweitzer of Lambarene, French Equatorial Africa. These pictures of him and his hospital work in the heart of needy Africa made a deep impression on Mr. and Mrs. William Larimer Mellon of Tucson, Arizona.   The pictures started a train of thought and action which led them to prepare themselves for medical work at Tulane University; into the membership of the Park Avenue Christian Church, New York City; and to establish a hospital in the Artibonite Valley in Haiti at a cost to them of $1,500,000.

Life magazine gave the entire issue of December 26, 1955, to the history of Christianity. They requested the late Paul Hutchinson, editor of *The Christian Century,* to write the article. The article was well written and made a deep impression on all who read it. This special issue, dealing with Christianity, did not contain even one liquor advertisement. Evidently the editors felt that liquor advertisements, of which there are many in the regular issues of *Life,* somehow were not appropriate in this special number dealing with Christianity.

The Protestant Episcopal Church in a formal statement said recently, "When the eye-gate and ear-gate of the City of Mansoul are open, God enters through what is seen and heard; the trumpet sounds; the day star arises in our hearts and we become obedient servants and mediators. This is communication and communication is the chief business of the Christian Church. All through the ages the urgent priority has been 'by all means' let the message be heard. The twin miracles of radio and television enable us to go through closed doors and speak to men in the intimacy of their own homes, and give a fleeting opportunity to reach those who seldom give the church a chance to be heard."

Chapter 10

SPIRITUAL RESOURCES FOR EVANGELISM

In the work of evangelism something more than mere human ingenuity and power is required. Jesus knew this. This is why he promised, "Lo, I am with you always, to the close of the age." (Matthew 28:20.) The sender promised to be with the sent in this great business of making disciples. A heavy load cannot be moved by a thin copper wire attached to it. It will break. However, if the wire is attached to a dynamo it can move the load, not because of *its* ability to hold together, but rather because of the ability of the electric power flowing through it. This business of evangelism requires the power of God working through dedicated Christian men and women. They must ever be the channel through which divine power works for the redemption of men and nations.

A ship comes into the Panama Canal from the Atlantic. A gate is in front of the ship. A gate falls behind it. A man in an unseen control room pulls a lever. In a few minutes the ship is lifted noiselessly to a new level. What is the explanation? Through the months, the rains have been falling high up in the hills. Down through creeks and rivers the waters have flowed into a large reservoir. The canal is in touch with the reservoir. When the lever is pulled, the waters flow under the ship with power sufficient to lift the ship to a higher level for further progress. This is what happens when Christians are in touch with the illimitable power of God. They are lifted by his power to new levels of thinking and acting for further progress.

The Holy Spirit

The first and most important spiritual resource for evangelism is the Holy Spirit. Jesus said, "You shall receive power when the Holy Spirit has come upon you." (Acts 1:8.) This promise was given by him before Pentecost. The Holy Spirit came as promised upon his first disciples on the day of Pentecost. He was given to the disciples for the purpose of witnessing "in Jerusalem and in all Judea and Samaria and to the end of the earth." (Acts 1:8.) Superhuman power, the Holy Spirit, was given for a superhuman task, the evangelization of the world. One cannot explain the evangelistic results of Pentecost and throughout the Book of Acts in the lives of the early Christians apart from the presence and power of the Holy Spirit. With Paul the source and secret of his power was the Holy Spirit. He states, "Christ has wrought through me . . . by the power of the Holy Spirit, so that from Jerusalem . . . I have fully preached the gospel of Christ." (Romans 15:18-19.) Again he states, "My speech and my message were not in plausible words of wisdom, but in demonstration of the Spirit and power." (1 Corinthians 2:4.)

And to Timothy, his son in the gospel, Paul writes concerning the Holy Spirit, "God did not give us a spirit of timidity but a spirit of power." (2 Timothy 1:7.) With deep significance, the New Testament associates the power of the resurrection and the power of the Holy Spirit, for Jesus Christ was "designated Son of God in power according to the Spirit of holiness by his resurrection from the dead." (Romans 1:4.)

It can be seen quite clearly, therefore, that in the early church, as described for us in the New Testament, the primary source of power was the Holy Spirit. He is also the source of spiritual power for Christians today. The power available to the churches of this century, by which they are to carry on their evangelistic work, is not found primarily in organization, methods, public relations, or money, but in the Holy Spirit.

One thing that always happens when a Christian possesses the Holy Spirit and the Holy Spirit possesses him, is that his witness is given boldly in behalf of Christ. On Pentecost the first manifestation of the presence and power of the Holy Spirit was this, "They were all filled with the Holy Spirit and began to speak" and what they spoke was about "the wonderful works of God." Peter, the Pentecost preacher, related in his sermon the story of Christ, his death and his resurrection, and called upon all those who heard him to make an immediate decision. There was an amazing response. The Holy Spirit then as now was a Spirit of tireless, unafraid evangelism.

Peter and John, possessed by the Holy Spirit, said to those who had put them in prison for preaching, "We cannot but speak of what we have seen and heard." (Acts 4:20.) The compulsion to preach is the first prerequisite of good preaching. Someone has said, "A man talks about the weather because he has nothing else to talk about. He talks about Jesus Christ because nothing else is worth talking about. That kind of compulsion comes only to those who have felt the power of Christ at first hand. Like men released from prison after all hope is gone, they cannot refrain from telling others about it, especially others who themselves are imprisoned."

The two great evangelists today, as always, are the Holy Spirit and the church. It is the Holy Spirit that prompts the message. On Pentecost the disciples were all filled with the Holy Spirit and spoke, "as the Spirit gave them utterance." It was the Spirit which made their message effective. They spoke with a holy boldness. Every conversion is begun by the Holy Spirit, continued by the Holy Spirit, and consummated by the Holy Spirit. It was the Spirit who sent Philip to preach to the Ethiopian on the road from Jerusalem to Gaza. It was the Spirit who took Simon Peter on his evangelistic errand to the house of Cornelius and who validated Peter's words there. It was the Spirit who directed Paul's missionary evangelism, inspired him to establish churches in many centers, and made all his work effective and fruitful.

And the church is also God's indispensable instrument for evangelism. "The Spirit and the bride say come." This is the invitation and summons of the church. "Come and see," said Philip to Nathanael. The real invitation of the church is not, "Come and see what the Lord has done for me" but rather, "Come and see the Lord." Our primary message is not *our* experience of Christ, as valuable as that may be to each of us, but rather it is Christ. The church's summons to men is to come and see Christ, to hear what he has to say, and to permit him to do what he and he alone can do for them.

In the early part of the nineteenth century, the most popular preacher in London was Edward Irving. He had come to London from Scotland with the conviction that it was his mission to reach the so-called "upper classes" and for some time in carrying out this mission he met with amazing success. Before long, however, there began to appear strange demonstrations which Irving and his followers believed were manifestations of the supernatural. After some bitter experiences the mission ended in disaster, but not altogether through Irving's fault. During the height of the demonstrations on one occasion a voice was heard under one of the galleries exclaiming, "I want a body." The voice could not be traced to any individual. Irving's followers believed that it was the voice of the Holy Spirit calling for a human body to dwell in.   Whatever we may think of the incident in Irving's chapel, the plain Christian truth is that the Holy Spirit is now and always "wanting a body."   In every Christian's body and also in the church which is the body of Christ the Holy Spirit longs to dwell.

In the New Testament the "Spirit of Christ" and the "Holy Spirit" are often used interchangeably.   Paul says,

> Any one who does not have the Spirit of Christ does not belong to him.   But if Christ is in you, although your bodies are dead because of sin, your spirits are alive because of righteousness.   If the Spirit of him who raised Jesus from the dead dwells in you, he who raised Christ Jesus from the dead will give life to your mortal bodies also through his Spirit which dwells in you.   (Romans 8:9-11.)

In the booklet, *Recapturing Pentecost,* Halford Luccock, formerly on the faculty of Yale Divinity School, states:

> What do we mean by the Holy Spirit?   One of the simplest answers is that the Holy Spirit is the present tense of God. This definition is inadequate but it does picture the truth enshrined in the words, "The Holy Spirit."   It affirms that God is here, now and active.   To believe in the Holy Spirit is to believe in a God not located back in the past or off in the future, but God in the present.

Another biblical scholar, William Robinson, when he was principal of Overdale College in Birmingham, England, and a lecturer on theology in the University of Birmingham, made this statement about the Holy Spirit:

> What is the significance of the coming of the Holy Spirit? Our clearest teaching on this important question is found in the discourses of our Lord in the Upper Room as re-

corded in John's Gospel from chapters 14—17. Our Lord informs his disciples that he is going away and that where he goes they cannot come. They are filled with consternation, as well they might be. Further, he informs them that it is expedient *for them* that he should go away. This is, indeed, baffling. Their hearts are troubled and they begin to ask questions. But he tells them that he will send them another Comforter, that is One who will make them strong together. It would appear that this Comforter is none other than his "other self" for he says, "I will not leave you desolate; I will come to you" and "you heard me say to you, I go away and I will come to you." (John 14:18 and 28.)

The Holy Spirit, then, is none other than Jesus' "other self." By his going away and the coming of the Holy Spirit, Jesus is universalized. In the flesh he was circumscribed and localized in both time and space. In the coming of the Holy Spirit he is universalized in both time and space; he is present everywhere and everywhen in his risen power. That surely is one reason why his going away was expedient for the disciples. They were now never to be away from his presence. It is through the Holy Spirit, the Spirit of Christ, the Spirit of God, that the Church is always in the presence of her Lord with all that that means in available power.

Prayer

Another resource for evangelism is prayer. Prayer is not power. It is the way to power. It puts one in touch with the unfailing resources of God. When anyone avails himself of access to God in prayer, he feels and knows that the power behind him is greater than the problems ahead of him.

Jesus Christ our Lord was a man of prayer.   He prayed often.   Many times he prayed alone and sometimes at night. The Syrian stars knew him well.   Before he selected the twelve apostles, he prayed.   Before he chose the seventy, whom he sent out two-by-two, he prayed.   He prayed before his crucifixion; he prayed in the Garden of Gethsemane; and he prayed on his cross.

The early church prayed.   In the fourth chapter is this remarkable statement which shows the results of prayer:

> And when they had prayed, the place in which they were gathered together was shaken; and they were all filled with the Holy Spirit and spoke the word of God with boldness.
>
> Now the company of those who believed were of one heart and soul, and no one said that any of the things which he possessed was his own, but they had everything in common.   And with great power the apostles gave their testimony to the resurrection of the Lord Jesus, and great grace was upon them all.   (Verses 31-32.)

All these things happened as a result of prayer.

Richard Chenevix Trench, in his well-known lines, says,

> Lord, what a change within us one short hour
> Spent in Thy presence will prevail to make!
> What heavy burdens from our bosoms take,
> What parched grounds refresh as with a shower!
> We kneel, and all around us seems to lower;
> We rise, and all, the distant and the near,
> Stands forth in sunny outline brave and clear;
> We kneel, how weak! we rise, how full of power!
> Why, therefore, should we do ourselves this wrong,
> Or others, that we are not always strong,
> That we are ever overborne with care,
> That we should ever weak or heartless be,
> Anxious or troubled, when with us is prayer,
> And joy and strength and courage are with Thee!

George A. Buttrick says:

> *Prayer* turns the event. It is a thrust into the movement of
> man's life. It is not merely passive resignation, but dy-
> namic power. Did not Archimedes say that if he could
> find a fulcrum—somewhere to rest his crowbar—he could
> move the world? Prayer is more than a fulcrum: it lays
> hold of the energies of God. The words of Jesus are not
> passive concerning prayer: "*Ask,* and it shall be *done.*"
> That language points to the very stuff of deeds.

Someone has said that he practiced prayer for the same reason
that he went to his oculist—to get his vision adjusted. Prayer
gives one the ability to see things in their proper relation and
perspective. It gets life into a proper focus. William Adams
Brown was one of the wisest men of his generation. He testifies
concerning prayer: "Prayer introduces us to the great companion who meets our human needs with his divine response.
The man who has learned to pray is no longer alone in the
universe. He is living in his Father's house." J. Hudson Taylor once said, "Do not have your concert first, then tune your
instruments afterwards. Begin the day with the Word of God
and prayer, and get first of all in harmony with him."

To pray for others is intercessory prayer. Jesus said to Simon
Peter, "I have prayed for you." To pray for others is one of
our highest and holiest evangelistic responsibilities. There are
those, and their numbers are large, who pray for others that
they may become followers of Christ, obey him, and serve him.
Many pastors and laymen carry a list of friends not members
of any church, for whom they pray. "More things are wrought
by prayer than this world dreams of," and one of the "more
things" is the conversion of others which is one of the results
of intercessory praying. A pastor once said to the writer, "I

have decided upon my own personal evangelistic responsibility for this Lenten season. I have worked out my prayer list, containing the names of the 'brothers-in-law' of my church. These are the men whose wives belong to the church and they do not. I expect to do my best by prayer and personal interviews to win these men and unite their homes for Christ."

Simon Peter was put in prison because he preached. Of this experience we read, "Peter was kept in prison; but earnest prayer for him was made to God by the *church*." (Acts 12:5.) Many churches have prayer cells or groups. One New York church has twelve such groups of about fifteen members each. They meet weekly. This fellowship of prayer is effective for evangelism. A Protestant Episcopal church in Pittsburgh has a number of prayer groups. One of the concerns of these groups as they pray is for the unreached of their community. Such praying creates a warm expectant atmosphere in a local congregation. One cannot grow seeds in frozen ground; neither can people be won to Christ in an atmosphere that is cold and indifferent. When Christian people really pray for others, something happens.

Under many different names and auspices, our day is witnessing the coming into being of thousands of small prayer cells or groups. These are a part of the present spiritual awakening in America. All great and lasting revivals of religion have been saturated with prayer. These groups are not something new. John Tauler's movement (Friends of God) and John Wesley's movement were both characterized largely by the number of small cells or groups which met regularly for prayer. They provided the major means of growth in the Christian life. Christians should not be afraid of the word "cell," just because the Communists use the word. However, long before there were Communists, the churches were using this word. A cell is an

organism within a living body. So widespread are these prayer
cells across the world today that one might almost say they are
a definite part of the new spiritual resurgence of our time. The
whole church benefits by the intensification and deepening of
the spiritual life through these prayer cells. One of the tests
of a prayer cell is that the members of it will, under the leadership and power of the Holy Spirit, be willing to be used of God
to answer their prayers. It is not enough just to pray. Christians must both pray and act. If they pray for their unchurched
friends, they must be willing also to speak their word of witness
and to extend an invitation to "come and see."

A praying revival is needed. One of the most heartening
things that have happened in America in recent years took place
at the first inauguration of President Dwight D. Eisenhower
when he led the nation in a prayer which he himself had
written. Many who heard this prayer were reminded of the
prayers of George Washington and Abraham Lincoln. There
is a renewed interest today in prayer, as indicated by the unprecedented use of devotional pamphlets, booklets, and books.
The Universal Week of Prayer which was organized over one
hundred years ago is observed annually during the first full week
in January. During World War II a "Minute of Prayer" was
heard daily over the radios of the nation. These prayers were
prepared by the Department of Evangelism of the former Federal Council of Churches. Station WOR in New York has
continued this daily "Minute of Prayer" because of so many requests. It seems to meet a need on the part of many in its listening audience. Today many councils of churches and local
churches provide, by means of the telephone, a "dial-a-prayer"
plan. The great number of people who dial and listen to a
prayer is amazing. There are many other days and weeks of
prayer within the calendar of the churches. Perhaps the most

widely observed and the best attended is the World Day of Prayer, sponsored and directed by United Church Women. This World Day of Prayer is held on the first Friday in Lent annually. In 1956 the day was observed in 143 countries and territories.

Many congregations, just preceding a week of visitation evangelism or a preaching mission, observe a twenty-four-hour vigil of prayer. Many general assemblies and conventions, held annually by the churches, provide for a prayer room which becomes a source of power for the delegates. Because of the inspiration, power, and fellowship that come through united prayer, it is not surprising to have the Apostle Paul say:

> Pray at all times in the Spirit, with all prayer and supplication . . . and also for me, that utterance may be given me in opening my mouth to proclaim the mystery of the gospel, for which I am an ambassador in chains; that I may declare it boldly, as I ought to speak. (Ephesians 6:18.)

The Bible

Another spiritual resource for evangelism is the Bible. It is the Book of all books. It contains the Word of life. Jesus said, "The words that I have spoken to you are spirit and life." (John 6:63.) The Bible is God's message to men. It is a lamp to our feet and a light unto our path. (Psalm 119:105.) It is the indispensable book for evangelism.

The Bible is the Book for all nations. It is the one book that appeals to all people and is read in almost all nations and is potentially available on a world-wide scale. This book has not been off the press for over 400 years. It has been translated and printed in over 1,100 tongues. It is a best seller year after year. Someone has said, "The Bible is a best seller year after year because it contains the answers for which modern man is searching. The teachings and insights of the Book are dateless, unhampered by time or space. Like the law of gravitation or the science of mathematics, it is not the source or place of origin which is most important, but the application of its truths." This fact can be illustrated by this incident: One day a mechanic was called to repair the mechanism of a giant telescope. During the lunch hour the chief astronomer, a rather sophisticated man, came upon this highly skilled mechanic reading the Bible. Obviously surprised he asked, "What possible good do you, of all people, expect to get out of reading the Bible? It is out of date and we do not even know for sure who wrote it."

The mechanic puzzled a moment, then looking up he asked the astronomer, "Don't you make considerable use of the multiplication table in your calculations?"

"Certainly," replied the sky watcher.

"Do you know who wrote it?" the mechanic queried further.

"Why, no, I guess I don't," the man admitted.

"Then how can you trust the multiplication table when you don't even know who wrote it?"

"Oh, that's easy," replied the astronomer with a degree of finality. "We trust it because . . . well, because it works."

"Exactly," replied the mechanic, "and I trust the Bible for the same reason—because it works."

Margueritte Harmon Bro describes the Bible as the "Book of our Fathers." She says:

A house in which a family has lived for two generations or more becomes filled with associations. . . . So, too, in a real and direct fashion the family Bible sustains each new generation. Not in the old way of family worship, perhaps. But this is the book which Father quoted on occasion— and to the point; this is the book which Mother was often seen to read. The children carried copies of it to Sunday school and off to college. Yes, and a little New Testament was slipped into the overnight bag when any member of the family went to the hospital for an operation. It *has* been a family standby and therefore it *is* a family standby. Somehow the Bible is not just one more book in a book-filled world. It's the only book we have ever read which we know for sure our grandparents read, too; and their grandparents, and theirs. . . . It's a family book.[1]

The Bible transcends time. Here is a library of 66 books written centuries ago in Hebrew, Greek, and Aramaic in a country about the size of Vermont State. These languages were spoken by hundreds of thousands of people and read by only thousands. Any other book with such a background would have been obsolete years ago. Even a popular novel rates a high place in annual sales for several years at the most. The Bible knows no limits of territory. It hurdles all national boundaries. The story of the present world-hunger for the Bible is one of the most encouraging and challenging developments of our time. In almost every part of the world, spiritually hungry people are having the Bible distributed among them. The Bible is not limited by tongues and dialects. For the past half century some part of the Bible has been appearing in a different language at the rate of about one every 32 days. When the Bible speaks to a people in their own tongue, they invariably hear in those words the will of God. "I am in that Book," said an African native. The Scriptures open the door not only to salvation but to literacy and thus to world culture. What can a man do for his brother that is more inspiring than to give him God's Word in his own tongue?

The annual circulation of the Scriptures has been growing steadily year by year. The present-day figures are amazing.

[1]From *Every Day a Prayer*, by Margueritte Harmon Bro. Used by permission of Harper & Brothers.

They show an average circulation over the last decade of more than 20,000,000 copies a year. To publish and circulate over 20,000,000 Bibles, Testaments, and Portions in a year is a staggering achievement and one that has no parallel in the realm of books. A new translation of the Scriptures was completed in September, 1952, by the American Standard Bible Committee of 32 scholars. This committee worked for 14 years to produce the Revised Standard Version. In four years, from 1952 to 1956 inclusive, 3,000,000 copies of the New Testament and 4,000,000 copies of the complete Bible were sold. According to the figures given out by UNESCO (United Nations Educational, Scientific and Cultural Organization), 3,000 languages are spoken in the world today. Of these only 190 have the complete Bible and another 937 have some part of it. Fully half the languages of the world do not possess so much as a single sentence of Scripture. There is much translation yet to be done, and also plenty of distribution work, too.

Columbus never explored all of South America, but touched it in only a few places on the northern coast; and yet he had no hesitation in pronouncing it a continent. As he looked upon the vast volume of fresh water rushing through the wide-mouthed Orinoco into the sea, he said, "The stream, comrades, never came from an island. I am sure that it has gathered its giant waters from a vast continent." When we contemplate the stream of blessing flowing from the Bible, we instinctively exclaim in the language of another, "This Book, so boundless in resources, never came from a created mind; it bears its own witness to its divine origin. Man is not its author, but man's Maker; its fulness betokens not the finite, but the infinite."

One reason why more people do not become members of the churches is because they do not know *how*. They say, "*How* do you become a Christian? What is required?" The source book, which gives the answer to these questions, is the Bible. Anyone who will read the Gospels and the Acts of the Apostles will find the answer to his question, "How do you become a Christian?"   Also, any minister or any other Christian who desires to lead another to become a Christian must refer to the Scriptures and say, "Christ says" and "the Bible says."   Here is to be found the source of our authority and here are the steps made very clear that are necessary for any person to take in order to become a Christian and a member of the church.   The New Testament is filled with many instances of conversion.   The same steps necessary for anyone to become a Christian in the first century, as recorded in the New Testament, are the same steps necessary for anyone to take in the twentieth century in order to become a Christian.   The gospel has not changed.   We have the same gospel now which was proclaimed in New Testament times and it is still "the power of God for salvation to everyone who has faith."   Anyone who studies thoughtfully the conversions recorded in the Book of Acts, will note that four things characterized conversion.   These were hearing the gospel; believing the gospel; repentance of sin; obedience in baptism.   Then followed God's part in conversion—forgiveness of sin; the gift of the Holy Spirit and eternal life.   If and when these four steps were taken in sincerity, a person became a Christian and a member of the body of Christ—the church.   This was but the beginning.   Then came the living of the Christian life which was a long and sometimes a difficult experience.   So today whenever and wherever the gospel of Christ is preached, taught, and lived, converts are made.

Clarence Hall of New York tells the story of a people he found at Shimmabuke.   He was a war correspondent in the South Pacific in World War II.   He visited a village on Okinawa. It was an obscure little community of only a few hundred natives.   Thirty years before an American missionary on his way to Japan had stopped there.   He did not stay long—just long enough to make several converts, leave a Bible with them, and pass on. One of the converts was Shosei Kina and the other, his brother Mojon. From the time of the missionary's visit they had seen no other missionary, had no contact with any other Christian person or group. But in those thirty years these two brothers had made the Bible come alive. Picking their way through its pages, they had found not only an inspiring person on whom to pattern a life, but sound precepts on which to base a society. Aflame with their discovery, they taught the other villagers until every man, woman, and child in Shimmabuke was a Christian. Here is evangelism growing right out of the Bible. Then after thirty years came the American army, storming across the island. Little Shimmabuke was directly in their path and took some severe shelling. When our American soldiers came into the village, the two little old men stepped forward, bowed low, and began to speak. An interpreter explained that the old men were welcoming them as fellow Christians. They remembered that their missionary had come from America. One sergeant said, "I don't understand it—people like this coming out of only a Bible and two old men who wanted to live like Jesus." Then he added, "Perhaps we've been using the wrong kind of weapons to make the world over." Mr. Hall concludes his story with this, "I can't help relating this story of Shimmabuke. I held in my own hands, for a few memorable moments, their Bible. At my request, Shosei Kina reverently took it down from the pedestal where it rested, handling it with the same loving care one would use with the original copy of our Declaration of Independence. It was weather-stained and frayed. Its covers were almost off, its edges dog-eared from thirty years' use. Carefully I turned its pages. I couldn't read a word of it, of course.   But I could read the inscription on the flyleaf.   It said, 'Published and distributed by the American Bible Society, New York.' "

Christian Fellowship

Another spiritual resource for evangelism is Christian fellowship.   On the first Christian Pentecost, the believers were separated into a church and bound together into a fellowship. It is said of them concerning their fellowship, "They devoted themselves to the apostles' teaching and fellowship."   (Acts 2:42.)   The Greek word for fellowship is *koinonia*.   Christians are a fellowship of the redeemed who belong to the body of Christ—the church.   Christian fellowship is of God and is sustained by our common experience of Jesus Christ our Lord. True Christian fellowship comes from above for "our fellowship is with the Father and with his Son Jesus Christ."   (1 John 1:3.)   This is the vertical dimension of fellowship.   There is a strength that comes to everyone who is in fellowship with other Christians in all lands.   This is the horizontal dimension of fellowship which begins ofttimes in a small group in a congregation, then widens to include the entire congregation, then the denomination, then other denominations at home and around the world.   The Christian's fellowship is one without frontiers for it extends to the throne of God and out to the farthest follower of Christ in the world.   Christians are those who not only believe something, but who belong to something.

This fellowship is interracial.   It knows no particular color of skin.   It leaps over barriers of languages, flags, customs, and nations.   Anyone who has attended ecumenical gatherings of Christians from over the world such as those held at Amsterdam in 1948 and at Evanston in 1954, realizes something of

the spiritual strength that comes from such a fellowship.   Often
this hymn of John Oxenham was sung:

> In Christ there is no East or West,
> In Him no South or North;
> But one great fellowship of love
> Throughout the whole wide earth.
>
> In Him shall true hearts everywhere,
> Their high communion find;
> His service is the golden cord
> Close binding all mankind.
>
> Join hands, then, brothers of the faith,
> Whate'er your race may be,
> Who serves my Father as a son
> Is surely kin to me.
>
> In Christ now meet both East and West,
> In Him meet South and North;
> All Christly souls are one in Him
> Throughout the whole wide earth.[2]

John Fawcett, a Baptist minister, wrote the hymn, "Blest
Be the Tie That Binds."   He was moved to do so because of
the reality of the love that bound the members of his congregation to him and him to them.   So strong was this tie that when
a more influential and a larger church offered him a much
higher salary, he refused the call because he found it impossible
to sever ties with those to whom he had ministered for so long.

When two Christians go together to win another to Christ,
they find strength in such a fellowship that is not experienced
if they go alone.   Here is to be found one of the values of a
preaching mission—the churches of a community work together
in an evangelistic fellowship.   The more inclusive this fellowship, the stronger it is and the greater the impact on the community.

---

[2]Quoted by permission of American Tract Society, New York City.

Church attendance strengthens this fellowship.   There is a renewal of spiritual life which comes through corporate worship.   Something happens in a congregation that prays and sings together; that listens to the same scripture readings and hears the same sermon.   Such an experience clarifies vision, inspires hearts, and strengthens fellowship.   When Christians absent themselves from the Lord's house on the Lord's day, they are in danger of committing spiritual suicide.   The Psalmist declared,

> I was glad when they said to me,
> "Let us go into the house of the LORD!"
> (Psalm 122:1.)

One reason for his gladness was the spiritual renewal he experienced when he worshiped with others in God's holy temple.

There is a spiritual fellowship to be found at the Lord's table, when Christians together partake of the bread which represents the body of Christ, and of the cup which represents the blood of Christ.   Horatius Bonar expresses our experiences at the Lord's table in a hymn:

> Here, O my Lord, I see thee face to face;
> Here would I touch and handle things unseen;
> Here grasp with firmer hand the eternal grace,
> And all my weariness upon thee lean.

> Here would I feed upon the bread of God;
> Here drink with thee the royal wine of heaven;
> Here would I lay aside each earthly load,
> Here taste afresh the calm of sin forgiven.

> I have no help but thine, nor do I need
> Another arm save Thine to lean upon:
> It is enough, my Lord, enough indeed;
> My strength is in Thy might, Thy might alone.

The question now comes to each Christian who has received this new spiritual strength: What shall I do with it? Surely some of it should be given to the business of evangelism, beginning with neighbors and friends and then extending to the uttermost parts of the earth. The power given on the first Christian Pentecost was not given for the ecstatic enjoyment of the disciples but it was given to them for the purpose of witnessing to others in behalf of Christ. Power was given for the purpose of witnessing boldly to their faith in Jesus Christ with the result that many believed and took their places within this divine-human fellowship called the church.

CHAPTER 11

THE SHEPHERD HEART OF THE CHURCH

One of the immortal songs of the Old Testament is the Twenty-third Psalm. We call it the "Shepherd Psalm." The books of Isaiah, Jeremiah, Zechariah, Ezekiel, and others of the Old Testament are filled with references to the oriental shepherd and his faithfulness to his sheep. The oriental shepherd did not herd his sheep; he led them. He was concerned for their hurts. He was the protector of his sheep, defending them against wolves and other deadly animals. He named his sheep and they responded to his call for "he calls his own sheep by name" and "the sheep follow him for they know his voice." The shepherds of Palestine, the land of the early ministry of our Lord, loved their sheep even unto death for "the good shepherd lays down his life for the sheep."

The last half of the Great Commission reads, "teaching them to observe all that I have commanded you." (Matthew 28:20.) New disciples are to be taught. They have entered Christ's school to be taught by him and of him. Each year, if a church is an evangelistic church, new members are added to its fellowship. Who has special responsibilities for their future teaching and training for the Christian life? This responsibility begins in most churches with the minister. Many times he is called "pastor." The term "pastor" means shepherd. The modern pastor is not a rancher but a shepherd. To do his best work he must possess the shepherd heart. This means a heart filled with tenderness and compassion. It is tragic when any pastor loses those qualities of heart that make him a faithful shepherd of those God has entrusted to him.

Principal James Denny of Glasgow said to a group of theological students on one occasion, "Don't become the pet lamb of your flock; be their shepherd." J. H. Jowett, a prince of the pulpit, once said, "The shepherd is to lead his sheep from the barrenness of the wilderness to green pastures and still waters. He is to watch against famine and drought. A flock is committed to a pastor's care. He is to defend the sheep against the perils of hunger. He is to find food for them. The pastor is responsible for the feeding of immortal souls. He is the guardian of the spiritual health of his flock. He is responsible for giving them the bread of life and the water of life."

Richard Baxter's congregation used to say, "We take all things well from one who always and wholly loves us." Some questions that present themselves to every pastor are: How much am I interested in the members of my congregation? How much do I *really* love them? Is my relationship to each member and to all the members professional or is there an indescribable love for every member? Usually the pastors who stay the longest in one church are the men who have the shepherd heart to the greatest degree. They have large capacities for friendship, sympathy, and fellowship. The members of a church have an uncanny way of knowing whether or not their pastor really loves them. Especially is this true of the children and young people in his membership.

While attending Drake University at Des Moines, Iowa, my pastor was Charles Sanderson Medbury who served this well-known church for many years. He was one of the city's first citizens, loved and honored by all. He had the shepherd heart.

He had a standing arrangement which the people of Des Moines understood. It was this—when he was at home, he left his porch light burning and anyone who wished to see him on any personal problem was welcome to come in and see him for an interview.

Some years ago at a drawing-room function, one of England's leading actors was asked to recite for the pleasure of his fellow guests. He consented and asked if there was anything special that his audience would like to hear. After a moment's pause, an aged minister arose and said, "Could you, sir, recite to us the Twenty-third Psalm?" A strange look passed over the actor's face. He paused for a moment and then said, "I can, and I will upon one condition and that is that after I have recited it, you, my friend, will do the same." Impressively, the actor began the Psalm. His voice and his intonations were perfect. He held his audience spellbound and as he finished, a great burst of applause broke forth. Then as the applause died away, the aged minister arose and began to recite. His voice was not remarkable; his intonation was not faultless. When he had finished, no sound of applause broke the silence, but there was not a dry eye in the room and many heads and hearts were bowed in reverential awe. The actor arose to his feet again. His voice shook with uncontrollable emotion as he laid his hand upon the shoulder of the aged minister, and said to the audience, "I have reached your eyes and ears, my friends. This minister has reached your hearts. The difference is this—I know the Twenty-third Psalm, but he knows the Shepherd."

The entire membership of a congregation must possess the heart of a shepherd. Everyone should feel a sense of responsibility for the care and nurture of others. By so doing, a fellowship is built up and strengthened. A sense of belonging as a member of a family is experienced.

There are two doors to every church.   There is the front door through which new members are brought into the fellowship of the church.   There is the back door which is to be kept closed. Unless it is kept closed, many members go out and are lost.

I preached one Sunday several years ago for the First Baptist Church of Hartford, Connecticut.   Upon the invitation of the pastor, Kenneth Maxwell, I remained for another meeting in the early evening.   To me it was a new kind of meeting which was held in the dining room and about the tables at 5:30 in the afternoon.   A light meal was served to about seventy persons. At one table sat thirty men and women who had been trained by the pastor to do the work of visitation evangelism.   That evening they were to go out two-by-two to call on about forty-five persons who were not members of the church but who should be.   These were the "front door" workers.

At the other table sat forty members who had been trained by the pastor to help him in shepherding the membership of the congregation.   They were sent out to call two-by-two in homes where there was sickness; where new babies had been born; where members were not coming to church, and where there were problems to solve.   This group was concerned about the "back door" of the church.   These two groups met together every Sunday evening for eight months out of the year.   Here is a great church which is concerned not only about those who are outside the congregation, but at the same time just as concerned about those inside its membership.

This church held no regular Sunday night services, except for the young people.   Therefore, the adults of the congregation were available for this two-by-two visitation program.   More churches, which have no Sunday evening services, would do well to imitate the First Baptist Church of Hartford.

Let us consider together the care of new members. This is a part of our evangelistic responsibility. The new members need and deserve the immediate care and constant love of the pastor and the congregation. How this is to be done and the degree to which it is done depend on the leadership—the pastor and officers—of the church. After an orange grove is planted, then what? Long months of cultivation, pruning, fertilizing, and spraying. After a baby comes into the home— then what? Long years of nurture, education, and training.

In these days when many congregations are having large numbers added to their memberships through a week of visitation evangelism or during a preaching mission, there must be careful planning for the care and nurture of the new members. This can be done and it is being done.

A long-time friend of mine, while serving as pastor in a church at Joplin, Missouri, invited an evangelist to help him in a preaching mission. After eight weeks of preaching night after night, 556 new members were added to the church. Most of these were first decisions. The pastor and evangelist realized before the mission closed that a tremendous responsibility rested on the pastor and his church for the nurture and care of these new members. The plan decided upon was that every Monday night for a year the new members were to meet together at the church. Only new members were permitted to be present. That year the pastor took no vacation. Before he left the city, the evangelist promised to return within a year. During the twelve months the pastor met the new members every Monday night as agreed upon. He conducted a Bible study at each meeting; he taught the new members how to pray and called upon many of them to pray publicly. He taught stewardship and asked each one to pledge weekly to the church. He taught missions and what this church's communion was doing at home and

in the far fields of the world.   He urged attendance at the church
school and at the worship services each Sunday.   The new members were urged to find others who were not members of the
church and try to win them to Christ.

At the end of the year, the evangelist returned as he had
promised.   He was amazed to find in the evening service all
but twelve of the 556 new members, and these twelve could be
accounted for by the pastor.   Six had passed away and several
had moved away.   What this faithful pastor did, others can do.
He was concerned about the back door as well as the front
door of his church.

Evangelism has a sequel and that sequel is the integration of
every new member into the fellowship and program of the
church.   The Protestant churches have never done better work
in the integrating process than now.   The great loss in membership today is not due to a failure by pastors and churches in the
care of new members.   The greatest place of leakage in membership losses is due to rapid removals of church members to
other communities and their failure to place membership in
a church of the community to which they go.

However, there are losses in membership due to our failure
to do better work in shepherding of the new members.   There
are holes in our fences through which many new members are
lost to Christ and the church.   One evening a grandfather was
relating a goodnight story to his little grandson.   The boy was
sitting on his grandfather's knee, listening intently to a story of
a lamb that got out through a hole in the fence and wandered
away in the field.   After a long search the shepherd found the
lamb.   It had almost perished.   He carried it home, cared for
it and, when it became well, he took it out and put it with the
sheep.   The grandfather started to get up from his chair and
take the lad to bed.   But the little fellow said, "Wait a minute,

Grandfather. Let me ask you a question. Did anyone think to go back and stop up that hole in the fence?" Good shepherding means more than that—it means feeding, watering, protecting, and nurturing. The Great Shepherd of us all says, "Feed my sheep" and "Tend my sheep."

What does integration of the new members into the life of the church involve? The answers to this are many, but let us consider a few major answers that are in the realm of the obvious.

Church Attendance—Young Christians need to worship weekly and corporately. Spiritual growth comes to them through fellowship with others of like minds and hearts. The loss of new members can be traced often to indifference to regular church attendance. Some of the responsibility for this loss can be laid at the door of the church. It is not always the new member who is at fault. Perhaps if our worship services were richer in content and more reverent and if the sermons were more helpful, the new member might not absent himself from the hour of worship on the Lord's day. All of us often excuse ourselves and place the blame on others for empty pews. We do well now and then to turn the searchlight on ourselves. We may be the problem. It may be that after the new member was "added to the church," no one called on him in his home, no letter was written to him, and no telephone calls were made personally for a talk with him. He was forgotten. It is time perhaps to give no less attention to putting saints into church windows but more attention to putting saints and sinners into empty pews. The most expensive piece of furniture in any church is an empty pew.

Recently the author heard of a strange family. The father has not missed church or Sunday church school in 23 years. The mother has had a perfect record for 11 years. The son has not missed for 12 years. A daughter has been teaching in the Sunday church school and has not missed for seven years. What is the matter with this family anyway? Don't they ever have company on Sundays to keep them from church? Don't they ever feel tired on Sunday mornings? Don't they ever have headaches or colds or sudden calls out of town? Don't they even have a radio or television in order to get some good sermons from out-of-town preachers? What is the matter with this family that it has such a faithful record in attendance upon the Lord's house on the Lord's day?

Bible Study—Every new member should own his own Bible. Many congregations follow the plan of presenting an inscribed Bible or New Testament to each new member at the time of being received into the fellowship of the church. Converts are far more receptive to teaching and training during the first year of their new church relationship than they are afterward. At the beginning they are willing to listen to what is expected of them.

Bible teaching can be done in three places. The first place to begin is in the home where the father and mother provide religious instruction. Many valuable helps are available to parents for such teaching. The denominational publishing houses have a wealth of material available for home instruction in the scriptures.

Bible teaching is to be found for the new members in the church school, whether conducted on Sunday or during the week. Our responsibility is to see that they are present regularly to receive this instruction. A shepherding church must be a teaching church. Trained teachers, excellent lesson materials, adequate physical equipment, and sufficient funds are necessary in order to maintain a high standard of teaching.

The pulpit is another place for the teaching of new members. Expository sermons will cause the membership of a church to "fall in love" with the Bible. It is said of Charles E. Jefferson that his sermons were so filled with scripture and scripture teaching that it was like taking a seminary course to hear them.

The Bible speaks today. The message of the Bible can never be silenced; it is eternal. Several years ago a renowned biblical scholar said that the Bible is "the most exciting book in the world. It looks at life frankly; glosses over nothing; and in page after page reads as if it were written yesterday." New members need to become intimately acquainted with this "most exciting book" for here is a source of spiritual strength for everyday living.

Daily Devotions—Daily prayer and Bible reading are essential for new members if they are to grow spiritually. A year's subscription to *The Secret Place,* or *The Upper Room,* or any other denominational daily devotional booklet or book is a valuable help to spiritual growth. A Chicago minister with a large church membership commits every member received into the church to the practice of daily devotions. He reports that 80 per cent of his membership attend the services of the church at least once each week. He states, "There is a very close relationship between the practice of daily devotions and regular church attendance." Many Christians feel the need of worship during weekdays in addition to corporate worship in the church sanctuary on Sunday. The redcaps at Grand Central Station in New York City feel the need for this, for every Monday, Wednesday, and Friday noon the redcaps, led by Redcap 42, meet on track 13 in an empty coach for thirty minutes of meditation and prayer.

When purchasing a watch from a Swiss jeweler in Geneva, a man asked the jeweler this question, "When is the best time to wind a watch?" His reply was, "In the morning in order that the watch may meet the jars of the day on a full spring." The Psalmist said,

O LORD, in the morning thou dost hear my voice.

(Psalm 5:3.)

Bishop Ralph Cushman of the Methodist Church has practiced daily morning prayer ever since he was a student in his seminary days. Out from this experience he wrote this poem entitled, "The Secret"[1]:

I met God in the morning,
When my day was at its best,
And his Presence came like sunrise,
Like a glory in my breast.

All day long the Presence lingered,
All day long he stayed with me,
And we sailed in perfect calmness
O'er a very troubled sea.

Other ships were blown and battered,
Other ships were sore distressed,
But the winds that seemed to drive them
Brought to us a peace and rest.

Then I thought of other mornings,
With a keen remorse of mind,
When I too had loosed the moorings,
With the Presence left behind.

So I think I know the secret,
Learned from many a troubled way:
You must seek Him in the morning
If you want Him through the day!

Weekly Giving—Early in their Christian experience, new members need to be taught "the grace of giving." They will not be offended if asked immediately after uniting with the

---

[1]From *Spiritual Hilltops*, copyright 1932 by Ralph S. Cushman. By permission of Abingdon Press.

church to make a weekly pledge.   These new members mean business.   They are anxious to give expression to their new spiritual experience.

There is a wealth of good literature on stewardship available to every church these days.   Some of it should be placed in the hands of new members in order to train them to be good stewards of Jesus Christ.   This means stewardship of life, time, and money.   A good place to begin with new members is to teach tithing.   G. Curtis Jones in his book, *What Are You Worth?* says:

> For approximately four hundred years following Christ's death, church leaders taught tithing as divine ordinance. In A.D. 585, the Synod of Macon declared that a follower of Christ who refused to pay his tithe should be "excommunicated" from the fellowship.   This fervidness of spirit "re-echoed" through the councils of the early church.   In A.D. 800, Emperor Charlemagne gave tithing virtually the status of law.   In the wake of the reaction against such legalism, tithing all but slipped out of Christian teaching, preaching and practice, until now we have gone almost to the opposite extreme.[2]

God owns all, we owe all.   God is owner, man is possessor. God is creator, man is custodian.   There is a vast difference between ownership and possession and new Christians need to be taught that distinction.   As possessors of that which we have, we are made God's stewards.   Some day we must give an accounting of our stewardship.   Not only are we called upon to give the one tenth to God, but we are responsible for the way we handle the nine tenths.   A man is known by the way he spends his money.

Jesus said, "You cannot serve God and mammon."   He might have gone on to say what is equally true—you can serve

[2]St. Louis: Bethany Press, 1954.   Used by permission.

God with mammon.   Martin Luther once wrote, "Every man needs two conversions—one of his heart and the other of his pocketbook."

Winning Others—New members are usually eager to tell others of their Christian experience and what it means to them to know and follow Christ.   When Andrew found Christ he turned at once to find his brother Simon Peter.   "He brought him to Jesus."   The Samaritan woman discovered Christ.   At once she returned to her city saying to her friends, " 'Come, see a man who told me all that I ever did.   Can this be the Christ?'   They went out of the city and were coming to him." (John 4: 29-30.)   Then this happened when they saw and heard Christ for themselves, " 'It is no longer because of your words that we believe, for we have heard for ourselves and we know that this is indeed the Savior of the world.' "   (John 4:42.)

To put a new member with an older member in visitation evangelism is a wise thing to do.   These new members are willing and eager to tell what Christ and the church means to them. Jesus said, "You are my witnesses."   New members should be given opportunity to witness to their faith.

Systematic Calling—There is no substitute for calling on the new members as well as older members of the church.   This means calling in their homes.   The pastor needs to have a regular calling program for himself.   The wise pastor will organize his parish along geographical lines and his members into groups for shepherding.   He cannot do all the calling, nor should he be expected to.   The officers of the church and others should be ready to assume this responsibility.   One large parish at the heart of an American city has its membership divided into forty geographical groups.   Over these groups are lay leaders.   One person is made responsible for ten.   Thus nearly 250 people in this one parish share in the pastoral ministry of the church.   A church, small in membership, can follow this same parish plan.

Membership Classes—Most churches have membership or catechetical classes for those who plan to become members of the church. The members of this class, old and young, are prepared to take one of the most meaningful steps of their lives and to do it intelligently. This is something that every church should do at least once each year. But there is a further step that can be taken in this matter. After the new members have been received into the church, there should be further teaching concerning the meaning of church membership. There are valuable booklets and books available to churches for this further teaching and training responsibility.

Let us take a look at the members who move. As has already been stated, our greatest loss in church membership comes from these rapid removals of individuals and families from one community to another. America is on wheels. People change addresses rapidly. Rural people are moving to the city. City dwellers are moving to the suburbs. Many, when moving from one place to another, fail to place membership in a local congregation in their new place of residence. Therefore they are lost to the church and in many instances they themselves become "lost." One authority on this matter stated recently, "Surveys in cities and towns across the nation reveal the fact that there are approximately as many members outside the church as inside in any given community." In a recent article by one of the ministers of Disciples of Christ, this statement was made:

> During World War II and immediately following, more than 600,000 members of our communion in the United States moved. This is approximately one-third of our resident membership. It is estimated that at the present time there are 250,000 of those who have moved who have never affiliated themselves with any congregation in their new community. Thus there are enough nonresident mem-

bers of Disciples of Christ in the United States to constitute 500 churches of 500 members each.[3]

What is true with the Disciples of Christ is true of almost every denomination in America. The urgent need is for better
shepherding in behalf of those who move from one community
to another.

There are a number of churches, especially among those of
the American Baptist Convention and Disciples of Christ, which
follow a very valuable procedure when members move from one
community to another. It is a brief Godspeed service, for those
who are about to leave the congregation for a new home in another part of the country. They are invited to stand before the
chancel prior to or following the sermon in the worship service.
The minister or some official of the congregation expresses appreciation in behalf of those who are leaving; recognizes the con-
tribution they have made to the church; wishes them Godspeed
in their new community and urges them to take membership immediately in some church in their new place of residence. Many
churches have found such a Godspeed service very valuable as a
part of membership conservation when Christians move to another community.

James F. Rowan, general manager of the Movers' Conference
of America, tells us that the two largest interstate moving companies alone did approximately the same amount of business
in 1954 as the top 50 did in 1947. When vans or trucks move
people at the rate of one in five persons per year, is there any
wonder that the churches have a problem in relocating "the
lost sheep"?

What can be done to solve this problem of conserving our
church members who move?

---

[3]Harry M. Davis from "Must We Lose 250,000 Disciples," from *The Christian-Evangelist,* January 4, 1949. Used by permission.

Select a committee on nonresidents. The members of this committee should be men and women who are interested in this problem and who feel a responsibility for those who have moved to a new community.

Secure the names and addresses of the nonresident members through every possible avenue of approach to the problem.

Get in touch with the nonresident members through letters.

Notify the minister of the church nearest the member, asking that he contact him and discuss with him his church membership.

Contact the local nonresident members to enlist them in the work of the church. Many of these can be discovered through a census, a "welcome wagon," telephone and gas companies, and in other ways.

One communion has designated February of each year as "nonresident-members month." At this time a special effort is made to persuade every nonresident member to become identified with a church in the community in which he lives.

In a survey in Washington, D. C., which was made by expert leadership several years ago, it was discovered that if a church member moved into the nation's capital from some other community and did not place his membership in some church within six months, he was lost permanently to the churches of the city. What is true of Washington holds true in many other cities across America. This tragic situation is due partly to a lack of understanding as to the meaning of church membership. It is due also to our poor methods used in the transfer of church members. Often new members are given the impression that when they unite with the church on confession of faith and baptism, they are uniting only with that particular *local* church. How much better it would be for the new members and for the church if they were taught that in becoming a Christian they thereby become a member of the body of Christ—his *universal* church; that the church is a glorious world fellowship and that they are a part of this fellowship, and no matter where they move, they are to remain faithful until death to Christ and his church. Most of our present teaching gives the new convert the idea that he is joining just a local church and when he moves away from it, he is not obligated to accept responsibility in any other congregation until he is formally received into some other local church. As long as we continue to give a narrow interpretation of church membership to new Christians, the situation will not be any different than it is today. Our staggering membership losses will continue.

Some good questions for pastors and churches to ask themselves concerning this great business of assimilation of new members are these:

> Is our interest in getting members into our churches only so that they may help us locally with the budget; or is our main concern that they may be blessed of God by entering into a saving relation with him?
>
> Is my church willing to take time to write a letter and spend three cents for a postage stamp in order to notify some pastor or church within the new community where some member of my church has moved?
>
> Is there not a need these days for focusing the attention of the church upon the worth of the moving member that would cause it to write, as did Paul to a sister church, saying, "I commend to you . . ."?

One of the deathless parables of Jesus is the one concerning the shepherd with 100 sheep. One became lost. Jesus said, "What man of you, having a hundred sheep, if he has lost one of them, does not leave the ninety-nine in the wilderness, and go after the one which is lost, until he finds it?" (Luke 15:3-4.) This parable is a window through which we can look at the shepherd heart of Christ. The word in this parable that should haunt the pastor of every church is this word *until*. Do my church and I have this kind of a shepherd heart? Are there inactive members on the roll? Then the search must be kept up *until* the lost is found.

How appropriate for us today are the words of our Lord to Simon Peter when he said to him:

> "Simon, son of John, do you love me more than these?" He said to him, "Yes, Lord; you know that I love you." He said to him, "Feed my lambs." A second time he said to him, "Simon, son of John, do you love me?" He said to him, "Yes, Lord; you know that I love you." He said to him, "Tend my sheep." He said to him the third time, "Simon, son of John, do you love me?" Peter was grieved because he said to him the third time, "Do you love me?" And he said to him, "Lord, you know everything; you know that I love you." Jesus said to him, "Feed my sheep." (John 21:15-17.)

One of the tests of our love for Christ is to be found in our work of shepherding. Peter never forgot this confrontation experience with his Lord. In his first epistle he says this, "For you were straying like sheep, but have now returned to the Shepherd and Guardian of your souls." (1 Peter 2:25.) Again the apostle says a little farther on in the same epistle, "Tend the flock of God that is your charge, not by constraint but willingly, not for shameful gain but eagerly, not as domineering over those in your charge but being examples to the flock. And when the chief Shepherd is manifested you will obtain the unfading crown of glory." (1 Peter 5:2-4.)

CHAPTER 12

EVANGELIZING TOGETHER

On November 11, 1936, the bridge which spans the bay between San Francisco and Oakland was dedicated. At that time I was directing the Bay Area Preaching Mission. One of the engineers, who helped build the bridge, showed me a sample of the cable that was holding it up. Said he, "In this cable are 17,500 wires. Each wire has a tensile strength sufficient to hold up a Ford car. Of course, no one wire can hold up the bridge, but all these wires working together are holding up the bridge and will carry the traffic through the years." Here is a lesson on Christian co-operation for the communions with reference to their evangelism. No one communion, no matter its size, can evangelize America by itself. It is a task for all the churches to undertake together.

The evangelization of America, or any one of its communities, calls for a two-lane evangelistic highway, with the traffic all moving in one direction. One lane is the denominational lane and the other is the interdenominational lane. There are times when the churches of one communion need to proceed along their own lane by themselves in their evangelism. Each communion today has its own evangelistic program for its own churches. These programs are more adequate and effective than ever before. Then there are times when all the Protestant churches of a community and across the nation need to move over into the interdenominational lane for a time and proceed together in order to engage unitedly in one or more evangelistic projects.

Prior to 1912 the communions had not learned to act together in evangelism except in union revival meetings. In the Charles G. Finney, Dwight L. Moody, Billy Sunday, J. Wilbur Chapman, William Biederwolf, Sam Jones, and Gipsy Smith revivals, they worked together on a community level.

After the organization of the Federal Council of Churches in Philadelphia in 1908, evangelism became a co-operative enterprise. It was in 1912 that the Commission on Evangelism was organized as a part of the framework of the Council. It was not until October, 1918, that the commission called a full-time executive secretary in the person of Charles L. Goodell of New York City. He served the commission for sixteen years. During his tenure, the budget of the Commission on Evangelism was the smallest of any unit in the Federal Council and was never more than $15,000 in any one year. It should be said in all fairness to the Council that the days from 1912 to 1930 were days when evangelism was not at the center in the plans and programs of most of the communions which made up the Council. Evangelism had become marginal. In those days, many pastors and educators were allergic to the word "evangelism." In some circles the term was not used. It is quite difficult in these present days, when evangelism is so much at the heart of the plans and programs of the communions, to realize that it has not always been so.

Up to 1932, only two communions had full-time secretaries of evangelism. One of these was the Presbyterian Church (U.S.A.) and the other was Disciples of Christ. The situation is entirely different now. At the present time there are about forty-six secretaries of evangelism in 35 Protestant communions. These communions provide their evangelistic leaders with definite budgets with which to carry on their work. They maintain national and area offices. The staff of the Department of Evangelism of the National Council of Churches of Christ in America now numbers six full-time men with a 1956 budget of $154,710. In a quarter of a century, evangelism has been brought from the edges to the center in the life of the American Protestant churches. When a large flywheel in a factory is centered perfectly, it is rhythmical and powerful. But when it gets off center, the results are disastrous. It will shake both itself and the building to pieces. When a local congregation, a denomination, or a council of churches makes and keeps evangelism central, the greatest spiritual and numerical progress is made.

This is a time for all the churches to co-operate more closely than ever before. In unity there is strength. Aesop tells the story of a father whose six sons were quarreling one day. Stepping into their midst, he taught them a lesson in unity they never forgot. He gave the youngest son a bundle of sticks and asked him to break it, but he could not. He next gave it to a second son who tried to break it but with the same result. The bundle of sticks was passed around among the six sons. Not one succeeded in breaking it. Then the father took the sticks and told the boys that he would show them how to do it. He untied the leather thong which held the sticks together. Then one by one he took the sticks in his hands and broke each quite easily. As he did so, he said to his six sons, "My boys, as long as you stand individually you can be broken easily by your enemies, but when you stand unitedly you will be strong enough to overcome any adversary."

This is no time in the life of our nation and the world for the practice of isolationism or provincialism on the part of any local congregation or a communion.   Bishop Brent was right when he said, "The world is too strong for a divided church." There is no place for starring in evangelism on the part of any minister, congregation, or communion today.   Let Hollywood have the stars.   Co-operation and unity are the words for this hour.   God is moving today and unmistakably in the area of a larger co-operation and unity among his people.   Since God is moving in this direction, it is imperative that every Christian and each church catch step with him.

A man had a few goldfish in a glass bowl in his home.   In the spring of the year he dug a large pond at the rear of his home. He filled it with water.   When the water reached the right temperature, he carried the goldfish out to the pond and gently put them into the water.   They had been so accustomed to swimming around in their small bowl in little circles that they continued to swim in the same small circles in the pond.   But, it was not long before they discovered that the whole pond was theirs.   The whole pond of Christianity belongs to all the churches.   Martin Luther does not belong to the Lutherans alone.   He belongs to us all.   Likewise, John Wesley does not belong to the Methodists alone; or John Calvin to the Presbyterians; or Roger Williams to the Baptists; or Alexander Campbell to Disciples of Christ.   These and all other leaders in the various communions belong to us all.   So it is in evangelism. Whatever one communion has that is good, should be shared and it is being shared today as never before.   It is heartening to know that all the secretaries of evangelism of the Protestant communions of America meet for one entire day twice annually for prayer, fellowship, and a mutual exchange of insights, ideas, plans, and literature. Then twice annually these same men, together with the appointed representatives of thirty communions, meet to give consideration to the plans and program of the Department of Evangelism of the National Council of Churches. On each day, when both the secretaries and the Department meet, the chairman of the Department presides. Over the years these exchanges of ideas, methods, and literature have been so widespread that it is really difficult to tell one denominational program of evangelism from another. The methods used are almost identical. It is heartening to know that there is no area in the life of the Protestant churches today where there is more serious and wholehearted co-operation than in the area of evangelism.

There are more things the Protestant denominations can do together and better in evangelism than they can do separately. The following are some of these projects that are being done together now, some of which will be continued for some time to come and new ones added.

Religious Census—No one congregation or any one denomination should undertake a house-to-house census of its community alone. This is something for all the churches to do together. One of the most important factors in conducting a census is preparation. At least six months should be spent in getting ready for a community-wide, house-to-house census. It takes at least this long to enlist, organize, and instruct the workers; to order the literature needed; and to make the geographical assignments to each congregation.

Another important item with reference to taking a community census is that it should be taken with some definite purpose in view. Why is the census to be taken? What is to be done with the results after the census is taken? For example, the churches may decide to take a census preceding a week of visitation evangelism, a preaching mission, or as an integral part of a national Christian teaching mission.

In 1940 a preaching mission was held in Washington, D. C. This mission was to be preceded by a week of visitation evangelism in order primarily to secure the names and addresses of all those living in and around Washington who were not affiliated with any local church. Some months before these two projects were to take place, a census was taken. In Indianapolis also, a week of visitation evangelism and a preaching mission were held in 1953. As a part of the preparation for these two projects a county-wide census was taken on Sunday afternoon, December 7, 1952. The Roman Catholic church, the Jewish synagogues, and the Protestant churches co-operated in this huge undertaking. There were 9,110 workers enlisted who made 129,295 census calls. Of these many calls, only 2,865 declined to give information. It was a 94% coverage of the entire county on one Sunday afternoon. The tabulation of results indicated that there were only 22,629 persons who expressed "no church preference." The number of persons reported who were members of, attended, or preferred a Protestant, Roman Catholic, or Jewish place of worship in Indianapolis and Marion County, was 234,457. A total of 91,185 persons claimed interest in or preference for some church, but were not affiliated with any church in the county. A further breakdown of the figures indicated that the committee turned over to the Methodist Church the names and addresses of 21,332 who preferred the Methodist Church but were not members of any church of that communion in the county. There were 14,880 such names given to the Baptists; 11,536 to Disciples of Christ; 6,096 to the Presbyterians and 2,314 to the Evangelical United Brethren.

Most leaders in evangelism agree that because of the rapid shift in population across America today, a house-to-house census should be taken unitedly in a community once in every three or five years. Census materials may be secured from almost any one of the denominational publishing houses or from the Department of Evangelism of the National Council of Churches.

Christian Ministry in the National Parks—One of the most unusual and effective programs being conducted through the Department of Evangelism of the National Council of Churches is a united program called "A Christian Ministry in the National Parks." There are about 15,000,000 persons who visit the National Parks in America each year. A few of these National Parks had weekly religious services prior to 1952. Now through this united program of the denominations represented in the National Council of Churches, a ministry is provided this year (1956) in 23 National Parks, located in 11 states and Alaska. The program is conducted this year by 110 young ministerial and college students—both men and women—who represent 23 communions, 25 seminaries, and 50 colleges. Each student is required to attend a two-day training course. These students conduct both Sunday morning and evening services of worship. During the week they hold campfire powwows and songfests for the younger generation. They also conduct daily vacation Bible schools and hold evening vesper services. These student workers are a moral and a spiritual force in every Park where they work. Vacationing Americans have a unique opportunity each year to worship God in the natural setting of his creation.

University Christian Mission—No one communion in America can get on a tax-supported campus by itself to carry on a religious program. However, when the communions all go unitedly they are able to do so. These missions are called by various names locally, such as "Religion in Life Week," or "Religious Emphasis Week," or "Religious Focus Week." On the national level the name used is the "University Christian Mission." These missions were started in 1938 by the Department of Evangelism of the former Federal Council of Churches. During the first two years of these missions, 44 campuses were visited. Since 1938 over 300 missions have been conducted and financed by the Department of Evangelism. An average of 120 speakers have participated annually. These have received only their travel expenses for their services. An average of 22 missions have been held annually on the campuses of municipal, state, and church-related educational institutions. Where the Roman Catholics and the Jews participate a trifaith, not interfaith, arrangement is followed. This trifaith plan, where and when the Roman Catholics and Jews participate, seems to be very acceptable to the college and university administrations.

Just as the churches follow their young men and women in the armed forces through their chaplains, so the churches follow their young people to college in various ways, one of which is through the University Christian Mission. Long ago John Witherspoon, who was one of the presidents of Princeton University, said, "Every gownsman is a potential legion for God."

National Christian Teaching Mission—It was in 1945 that a series of missions to Sunday school teachers was conducted jointly by the International Council of Christian Education and the Department of Evangelism of the former Federal Council of Churches. These missions were initiated by the Department of Evangelism. After two years these missions were expanded in purpose and program into the National Christian Teaching Mission. One of the most effective instruments for evangelism is to be found in these missions. From 1947 to 1956 a total of 249 missions have been held. About 6,293 congregations representing most of the denominations have participated. This is an average of 25 congregations for each mission. These missions are held in both urban and rural areas. A religious census is a definite part of each mission, in order to discover the unreached in a community. In these 249 missions held thus far, the census has been taken in communities having a total population of 20,440,000. About 5,000 guest leaders have participated in these missions which are one week each in length. Each congregation is expected to invite its own guest leader to be present for the week to help the pastor carry out the mission program in his church. These guest leaders serve for their expenses only. In each mission, meetings are held with pastors, church school teachers, and other Christian education leaders. Plans are worked out also, for a follow-up on the census. A church school enlargement program is presented to each church for its consideration and action as a continuation of the mission. These missions are held under the sponsorship of the Department of Evangelism of the National Council of Churches in co-operation with local councils of churches.

National Preaching Mission—The story of the preaching missions in America is fascinating. The idea was first proposed by Hugh Thomson Kerr of Pittsburgh in 1934 and brought by him to the Home Missions Council, which referred the whole idea to the Department of Evangelism of the former Federal Council of Churches. For several years there had been a growing feeling within the churches that America needed a spiritual awakening. A carefully chosen committee was appointed which, over a period of 18 months, met frequently to select speakers, arrange a schedule of cities to be visited, formulate the program, and perfect organizational plans.

These missions, conducted interdenominationally under the Department of Evangelism of the former Federal Council of

Churches, began in September, 1936, with the writer as the National Director. Forty-one strategic centers, from coast to coast and from the Great Lakes to the Gulf, were visited in two years. Four consecutive days were spent in each city. More than 100 distinguished missioners participated, some serving for three months, others for two, others for one month or a lesser period. All served for their travel expenses and entertainment only. By this unselfish service, the dollar mark was removed from evangelism. In some places and by some "professional evangelists" evangelism had been overcommercialized. This is one reason why evangelism fell into disrepute some forty years ago.

The mission teams, during those first two years and since, have averaged about fifteen speakers. The largest number of speakers was used in the Greater Kansas City Mission, when forty men and women were members of the team and they kept 451 speaking engagements. So faithful were the speakers to their assignments that not one appointment was missed.

During these first two years of the preaching missions thousands attended. The largest auditoriums were packed out at night. There were meetings in each mission for ministers, luncheons for women, six simultaneous seminars for everyone, meetings with organized labor, service clubs, high schools, colleges, and in prisons. It was the purpose of these missions not to overlook any group in the community.

Never in the history of the churches in America had such a religious impact been made in such a brief space of time. These missions strengthened the foundations of Christian faith in the nation; they served to place evangelism at the heart of the program in the churches; they presented the gospel unitedly as one message; they marked a forward step in the realization of a closer co-operation and unity among the churches; and they brought a season of spiritual refreshing as from the Lord. These missions have continued from 1936 to the present time. They need to be continued indefinitely. Those who were a part of these preaching missions at the beginning in 1936, are unanimous in feeling that this united, aggressive evangelistic effort on the part of all the Protestant churches, was the inauguration of a new and a better day for Christ in America. The spiritual tides began to come in. When the tide comes in, it lifts all ships in the harbor. This incoming tide of evangelism lifted such ships as wor*ship,* fellow*ship,* steward*ship,* and Christian partner*ship.*

The day of the "revival meeting" is not over by any means. In fact, there are more such meetings being held now than ever before in America. Some are conducted by the local congregation with the pastor doing his own night-by-night preaching from one to three weeks. At other times, a guest pastor is invited to do the preaching, and at still other times pastors exchange meetings.

There are a few present-day and well-known evangelists who give full time to the holding of these "revival meetings" or "evangelistic crusades." The best and most widely known of this group of full-time evangelists is Billy Graham. His "evangelistic crusades," to use his own term, are six to eight weeks in length. The largest hall in a community is secured. Weather permitting, many crusades are held outdoors beneath the stars and under floodlights in a stadium. Many weeks are spent in preparation for each crusade. Special emphasis is placed on prayer as a definite part of the preparation. Considerable sums of money are spent on publicity, which is necessary in order to secure the attention and attendance of the community.

This young evangelist is preaching to more people every year through his night-by-night crusades—also by means of the radio, television, printing press, and films—than any other man in the world. All of his crusades are interdenominational and many times they are held under the sponsorship of a local council of churches. Billy is on salary. His team, on which there are about 10 members, is on salary. The local committee handles the offerings and gives a public accounting of just how the money is spent. All the team members are sincere and devoted young men.

Billy has his critics. Every well-known and successful evangelist has had them, hence this is not something new or unusual. But Billy's friends far outnumber his critics. No one, whether friend or critic, has ever doubted his sincerity or his devotion to Christ or his love for the church. His evangelistic messages are Bible-centered and Christ-centered. Emotionalism is absent from his preaching. Through his crusades he is reaching many whom the churches are not reaching.

Billy and his team were invited by the Protestant Council of Greater New York to hold an evangelistic crusade. This crusade will begin on May 15, 1957, and will continue for eight weeks in Madison Square Garden which seats 20,000. The last such united evangelistic effort on the part of the New York City churches was held by Billy Sunday about forty years ago.

Other well-known evangelists who are giving full or part time to revival meetings are E. Stanley Jones, Bryan Green (England), Alan Walker (Australia), Charles B. Templeton, and Charles and Laurie Taylor. Without exception, these men would agree that the present-day revival meeting or evangelistic crusade or preaching mission, where the Christian message is presented night after night, is not the most effective method by which to reach the unchurched of America. The audiences are made up of persons of whom 95% to 98% are members of some church already. Church members need these revivals which often bring a spiritual awakening within an entire congregation. Many who respond to the public invitation at the close of the message any evening are church members who desire to make a new commitment of themselves to Christ.

It is my own feeling that every local congregation should hold a revival meeting or Christian mission every two or three years. Each city should hold a united, well-prepared, Christian mission for one week or more every five years. In these Christian missions held by a team of speakers, or in an evangelistic crusade held by a full-time evangelist for six or eight weeks, some of the results are the presentation of a united Christian witness to the community by the churches; a renewal of the moral life of the community; a spiritual awakening of the membership of the churches; and the winning of new disciples for Jesus Christ.

In order for any evangelistic plan or program to succeed, long and careful preparation is necessary, thorough organization is needed, good music is required, and faithful preaching of the Christian gospel is an imperative.

Methods are not sacred. Truth is. Any church should be willing to discard an evangelistic method any time in order to supplant it by a better one. The important thing is to decide on some method or methods by which the unreached can be won to Christ and the church and then use them aggressively.

Visitation Evangelism—This is another effective method in evangelism which can be, and more often should be, done together by the Protestant churches of a given community. The plan usually followed in this united effort is to invite someone in from the outside to be the director of the program. Such a united program in lay evangelism may be carried out on the community or state level. Almost without exception, ministers of all communions are united in their feeling that here is one method of evangelism in which they can participate without any reservations.

In a week of visitation evangelism which usually begins on a Sunday afternoon and concludes on the following Thursday evening, each congregation selects its own workers and gathers its own responsibility list.   The plans and program are under the guidance of a local committee composed of the minister and one or two laymen and laywomen from each participating congregation.   The committee decides upon the place where the ministers and layworkers of all the churches are to meet on a Sunday afternoon for their first period of instruction.   It arranges for the evening meals, the ordering of the literature, and other matters having to do with the week's program.

In the church dining room where the Monday-to-Thursday evening suppers are served, each local congregation is assigned a table for its workers.   Following the evening meal, the director gives additional instruction to the workers with reference to the most effective ways to conduct their interviews.   Reports are made at the supper table by a few of the teams.   Following the supper, the instruction period, and prayer, the workers go out into the community to call on definite persons whose names have been given them by their respective pastors.

Too much stress cannot be placed on adequate preparation. Six months to one year is necessary for best results.   Excellent literature on how to do this work unitedly may be secured from the Department of Evangelism of the National Council of Churches in New York City.   In some instances, the Protestant denominations of an entire state may unite to conduct a program of visitation evangelism within a specified time.

Preaching Missions in Army Camps and Naval Bases—During World War II and following, the Department of Evangelism of the National Council of Churches held many preaching missions in military installations. Teams of speakers were secured for this purpose. The number on the team was determined by the size of the military base. The speakers served for their expenses only, and the chaplains in each base were responsible for the rooms and meals of the speakers. These missions have been and still are a co-operative evangelistic enterprise on the part of the Protestant communions. They are being carried on today as they have been in the past, in order to help the chaplains do their work.

Rescue Missions—In many of our metropolitan centers there are rescue missions. They do a remarkable interdenominational work in evangelism. One of the best-known and most effective of all these missions is the Bowery Mission, in New York City. It has been ministering to men since 1879. This mission is owned and operated by *Christian Herald*. Daniel A. Poling is not only the editor of *Christian Herald* but also president of the corporation that directs the mission. There is an evangelistic service conducted every night in the year and also at noon most of the year. The down-and-out man in this mission, as in all other missions, is looked upon not for what he is, but for what through Christ he can become. The Bowery Mission points with pride to hundreds of men who have become leaders, business executives, missionaries, ministers of the Gospel, because at a moment in their lives when they most needed help, help was given freely.

Mission to Ministers—In 1953 the Department of Evangelism of the National Council inaugurated a Mission to Ministers. Two have been held each year—one at Green Lake, Wisconsin, and the other at Northfield, Massachusetts. The attendance in each place has averaged about 250. The ministers are urged to bring their families. The emphasis of the program for each week is on evangelism. The speakers are selected with this emphasis in mind. In each mission many communions are represented. These Missions to Ministers are being held, as they have been in the past, by the Department of Evangelism of the National Council of Churches.

American Christian Ashrams—Since 1940 these Ashrams are held under the direction of the Department of Evangelism of the National Council of Churches. They were begun by the Department. They have been and are conducted within the framework of the Protestant churches. They are of the churches, by the churches, and for the churches. They do not revolve around any one man. They do revolve around Jesus Christ. He is the center of each Ashram and the textbook is the Bible. These Ashrams are interracial and interdenominational. Much of their emphasis is on the enrichment of the spiritual life and how to be more effective workers in the local church.

Ship Chaplains—The furnishing of ministers for ships to act as chaplains is an opportunity for evangelism. A number of ships make no provision for religious services. The Department of Evangelism of the National Council of Churches began this service in 1952. It has the co-operation of many steamship companies. Some request chaplains for special cruises.

The Observance of Holy Week—The united observance of Holy Week services annually on the part of many communities is a moral and spiritual force. Some of these services are attended by large numbers. Speakers are carefully chosen. In most instances the radio and the television stations are made available to get the messages out to the community. One reason why these Holy Week services are so largely attended is partly because people like to see the churches united in some worthwhile enterprise.

Reformation Sunday—Increasingly the churches are observing this day unitedly in order to give a united Protestant witness to the community concerning the things they believe. The attendance at some of these united services in many communities is between 2,500 and 20,000. These services are helping many to know the reasons why they are Protestants and why they should remain Protestants.

World-wide Communion Sunday—The observance of World-wide Communion Sunday is held on the first Sunday in October. This has come to be one of the most significant days in the church calendar because it calls attention to our united fellowship in Christ at his table as Christians in all lands. This day has done much and will continue to do much more in giving to all Christians a sense of oneness in fellowship at his table. One of the purposes of the day is to secure the presence of every resident member of every local congregation at its own communion table. Union communion services on this day are not encouraged or contemplated. The interdenominational responsibility for the preparation for this day from the beginning has been placed on the Department of Evangelism of the National Council of Churches. The Department of Evangelism began this observance in 1940 with reference to its interdenominational emphasis and sponsorship.

The last Sunday afternoon in September is a time for calling on the resident membership of the church to commit every person to be present at the Lord's table on World-wide Communion Sunday. If and when this is done, an Easter attendance is experienced. Almost always the attendance commitment is made for every Sunday in October.

Church Attendance—October is Church Attendance Month and should be observed unitedly by the churches of the community. Many churches carry on a special attendance program in October annually and unitedly beginning with World-wide Communion Sunday. In America the months of July and August are vacation months. There is a letup and a letdown in most churches during the hot weather. In September, immediately following Labor Day, most people return from vacations for school and business. Rally Day in most church schools is held the last Sunday in September. The Christian education forces are encouraged to strengthen their organization and set goals for attendance on Rally Day.

There is in America at present a healthy church attendance increase. There has never been a time in the history of the nation when as many people were attending the worship services of the churches as now. Many congregations are having to conduct two worship services on Sunday mornings in order to care for their increasing attendance. It is not too much to claim, although there are no reliable figures to prove it, that 50% of the resident membership of the local churches are present at one or more meetings each seven days of the week. If this is true, then this is the highest record the churches have ever enjoyed in America. A remarkable organization known as "Religion in American Life" is helping to increase church attendance in the month of November each year.

There is a motive for evangelizing together which Christians sometimes overlook. This motive is found in the prayer of our Lord when he prayed, "I do not pray for these only, but also for those who are to believe in me through their word, that they may all be one; even as thou, Father, art in me, and I in thee, that they also may be in us, so that the world may believe that thou hast sent me." (John 17:20-21.) Here, the Savior of the world is praying for the unity of his disciples in all generations, in order that "the world may believe." The most compelling reason for Christian unity is not unity for unity's sake or unity for bigness' sake, *but* unity for the sake of evangelizing the world. Perhaps the price we are paying for a divided church is an unevangelized America.

Halford Luccock reminds us of an incident in the Old Testament when a group came to the River Jordan. Because they could not pronounce a certain word they were slain. That word was "shibboleth." He adds this warning, "Unless Protestants learn to pronounce a word they are undone. That word is of two letters. It is the word 'we.'" Just so. If America is to be evangelized there must be unity. We must evangelize together. To paraphrase a verse in the Psalms—

> "Behold, how good and how pleasant it is
>   when brothers 'evangelize' together in unity."